THE HUMAN GROUND
Sexuality, Self and Survival
Revised and Expanded Edition

The Human Ground
Sexuality, Self and Survival

by Stanley Keleman

Introduction by GAY LUCE
Afterword by PETER MARIN

Science and Behavior Books, *Palo Alto, California*

Revised edition. First printing, November 1975.
Published by Science and Behavior Books, Inc.,
P.O. Box 11457, Palo Alto, California 94306

Sexuality, Self, and Survival (Lodestar Press): first printing,
October 1971, second printing, September 1972. *The Human
Ground* (Lodestar Press): first printing, August 1973.

Designed by George Calmenson, Lodestar Press, Berkeley,
California
Typeset by Vera Allen Composition Service, Castro Valley,
California

Library of Congress Catalogue Number: 75-12453
ISBN: 8314-0047-1

Manufactured in the United States of America.

To Robert, my son,
to learn from my journey.

This book is from
my memories
of Kairos.

The Human Ground/Sexuality, Self and Survival is an integrated, revised and enlarged edition of earlier works, including two new chapters: "The Family Is a Living Body" and "Working With Groups."

Contents

Introduction

Stanley Keleman is a teacher of awareness in the classic sense. Out of his own experience he finds words and exercises to evoke insight and learning in others. Although he decries asceticism and symbolic systems that separate people from their life process, his own personal development has all the earmarks of what would have been called mystical in another era. His philosophy, generated by his experience, has many commonalities with that of Buddhist teachers. His deep faith is in nature, in the body as the vessel of the life process. As he says, we *are* our bodily processes.

His essential message is simple: be yourself, experience your bodily life directly. Simple, and how difficult! I wonder what kind of woman I would be if I were able to be fully myself. I feel I have been separated from my emotional self for many years—since childhood, slowly binding myself off like a mummy, in my own constrictive habits. Growth and change are inevitable with a real teacher. And growth creates unease. I find that as in adolescence, when I could no longer take for granted my biological state of being, and life situation, I have the upsetting realization that I am not the way I believed. Stanely spent a long period training in various disciplines, as well as in his own self explorations. In this book he states his indebtedness to bioenergetics, and emphasizes his view of life as an energetic process. But the book is not about bioenergetic techniques, nor about therapy. It is an initial taste of Stanley Keleman's developing philosophy, and teachings for personal wholeness.

The book is an expanded and revised edition of *The Human Ground* and *Sexuality, Self and Survival,* which were originally compiled out of a number of weekend workshops, and published by Lodestar Press, whose publisher, George Calmenson, has said to me "Stanley has begun to write a new psychology, a psychology without an unconscious, a psychology about the formative process."

We do, after all, form ourselves throughout our lives, shaping our bodies and our characters—although we may not be conscious of what we are doing. For example, we have choices of responses even as infants. We can reach out to a punishing mother, or withdraw and shrivel, or we can defy, or comply. Each choice helps to define our character. Later in life, the rigidly held pelvics or constricted throats will in turn restrict our ability to enjoy sexual pleasure or express our feelings. Just as we form our physical-character from moment to moment, our behavior and feelings express our values. Socially there is often a discrepancy between verbalized values and action. In the family, when a parent's stated values are contradicted by his action, the child understands the behavior as his model, and becomes confused when rewarded or punished for values that are merely words. One of the problems with the social values that most of us have learned is that they are antithetical to life, and do not come from our biology. The need to be heroic, to be successful or productive in the eyes of an organization often places high value on biologically unhealthy acts such as enduring constant rush, eating and sleeping and working according to a clock that is unrelated to one's needs.

In our formative process, most of us have been reacting to the culturally imposed rational system that extends from the environment of our hospital birth, through the efficiency system of our schools. Even in this environment we are still, by our reactions, forming ourselves.

This book talks to two important aspects of the formative process—our grounding, and our sexuality.

In *The Human Ground*, Stanley Keleman talks about the ways in which we take on self definition and the uprightness of independent life, and how this may or may not be grounded in one's natural being. In *Sexuality, Self and Survival*, using vignettes from workshops, he demonstrates how the central energy of our sexual nature becomes diverted, dissipated, blocked and warped by conditioned responses that may begin in the cradle or with toilet training. He points out something that is ironic in our sexually alert culture: full sexual union is probably rare among us civilized westerners, who almost never feel a full build up of excitement that is expressed in a way that expands the boundaries of the person, far from a "shudder in the loins." Sexual behavior is not separate from any other behavior: It is a culmination, or perhaps better, a demonstration of who we are.

Since our bodies say who we are, to the practiced

eye, they also reveal at a glance the nature of our sexual experience. As a participant in Stanley Keleman's workshops I have often been astounded by his instant perceptivity, and wondered: how can he look at a total stranger and begin to accurately describe his temperament, his sexual hang-ups, his parents, and habits? His answer is plain: look in the mirror, feel how you breathe, watch and sense how you stand up, sit down, move, speak. It is all there.

Because this book is like attending a composite workshop, it cannot be read for information by the mode of skimming we are all taught in school. It is better to absorb it, feeling oneself and one's own breathing and posture in the process of reading. The book may seem to be abrupt at times. Stanley's forceful narrative to the reader is suddenly punctuated by voices of women and men who have never been introduced or described. They are the participants. Typically, a person who was stepping forth to do special work would have put on a bathing suit so that his or her body would be more visible. Then, usually Stanley would recommend an exercise to mobilize the emotional energy, a strenuous posture, deep breathing, or perhaps kicking a bed. Because the narrative of the book was carefully edited to preserve the vitality of the workshop, but not to describe the endless details, the actual exercises are omitted. The reader is present at the revelatory moments, moments of learning.

One way to participate in the book is to keep feeling its basic emphasis, that we are our bodies, biological beings. This is basic, irrefutable. Many of us have survived our anti-biological culture by turning away from the messages of our bodies, from our sensations and feelings, and numbing and freezing ourselves into a mold of acceptability. But simultaneously we have shut off our biological juices, the energy flow of our lives, and we act out cultural substitutes. Many of us are unaware of our own process until, one day, we realize we are impotent or frigid, or we suddenly find ourselves afflicted with colitis, or hypertension, or somebody dies, or we ourselves face dying.

I grew up in a comfortable middle class professional milieu, in which most afflictions were considered tragic and unpredictable. People considered that they were the victims of troubles, or disease. Surely, in those days, it never occurred to me that I was forming myself, and that my choices of work, of people, and my physical reactions to situations, my patterns of feelings, expressed or withheld, were helping me to build my character, and with it, my own ailments. I thought that things were wrong inexplicably. After getting married, I did not live happily ever after. Indeed, I was dissatisfied with a life that looked outrageously perfect to the outside, socially and intellectually rich, a good husband, material comfort. I felt that I had to be very sick to be unhappy in such perfection. I remember a therapist attempted to help me adjust to the situation I had built for myself, but after millions of words I still was unable to be mindful of my own ongoing experience, or to see how I could begin to form new responses. I was certain I was a pathological case, and probably hopeless.

Years later, in a summer workshop in Berkeley, I felt a joyous recognition listening to Stanley Keleman put things together. The messages from my biological self had always been there, but I had not known how to listen.

Stanley is part of a growing movement in psychology and other "sciences" of health in which practitioners are moving away from defining people by pathological categories, and therefore they are no longer offering therapy so much as education in self healing, self forming. Like Buddhists, or teachers of Alexander method, Stanley emphasizes that our bodies are not separate from our minds. Nor are we sealed off within our skins, separate from the world and the people around us, if we are in contact with our feelings.

Like many people in our culture, I used to look for means of coming closer to some ideal. By becoming more perfect, somehow, I felt I would be happier. It had never occurred to me that the issue was not any of my goals, including happiness, but to be myself.

Stanley Keleman holds out no goals—such as a better aligned body, or fearlessness, or even lack of headaches. He merely asks us to listen carefully to our own process, minute by minute, and thereby come to know it. Who am I? I look in the mirror for an answer and am startled to see some of my life story reflected back at me, the tight jaws of a small defiant child, the constricted chest holding down explosive emotions. How did I get this way? Under what conditions am I tightening these muscles? *The Human Ground* and

Sexuality, Self and Survival offer two basic aspects of how I got to be the way I am and where I can go from here.

Large numbers of Americans must be hungering for this wholeness of philosophy and practice. Having cut ourselves off from our contact with the nature of which we are part, we feel atomized, in need of a new path. Thousands of people are now learning about the habitual patterns of their minds and emotions by practicing some kind of meditation. Thousands of others are studying or seeking instruction from gurus of other cultures, cultures in which the process of self knowledge and integration is not separated from philosophy, from metaphysics.

Stanley Keleman's approach is distinctly not metaphysical, nor does it use symbolism. It offers a path for expanding one's boundaries that relies largely upon listening to one's physical self that does not require any search for lost innocence, or an elaborate ladder of exercises, but can come through direct tuning to one's life process. Thus slowly a person may restore his instinctual integrity.

Stanley Keleman, like many Buddhist teachers, suggests that there is a wholeness of being, permitting no body-mind distinction, no distinction between matter and energy, or inside and outside. A person who can expand into experience will have a vast universe of feeling, a universe within that may match what scientists describe as the astronomical universe without. It is we who impose limits upon the immensity of experience, applying positive or negative labels, judging every experience by the lexicon of our conditioning. Our experience develops structure, and our structure limits our experience. Anyone who wants to do something about the limits of his own experience, who would like to regain more of the deep satisfaction of his own human experience, will be grateful for the opening that is offered in this volume, and for the unfolding of subsequent books.

Gay Luce
Berkeley, California
August 1975

INITIATION

"There is no real difference between structure and function; they are two sides of the same coin. If structure does not tell us anything about function it means we have not looked at it correctly."

ALBERT SZENT-GYOERGYI

Life Builds Structure

I HAVE an absolutely stringent and inflexible rule about reality. If I am in contact with myself, I am in contact with the world. The relationship that I have to myself is the relationship I have to my world. It starts with me.

I don't deal with inter-personal realtionships. I deal with your relationship to yourself, with helping you into more intimate connection with yourself—by working directly with your body. The way your body is, is the way you are. That is my working principle.

System-oriented scientists who need to see the body as a machine, in terms of genetic code, feedback systems, organ organization and biochemical systems with predictable programs, do not seem to grasp that life includes mechanics, that it is living that is structured—that structure is a living function.

Your body is the life process, is the living structure called you.

Who you are as you stand in front of me is who you are in the world, is how you perceive your world, is exactly how you have learned to deal with the world. Your past in hereditary as well as personal terms is living at this present moment, as you the body.

Your expression, your form is the movement and shape of your psyche. For me, the content of your psychic conflict is not the essential factor. The qualities of expression and its direction are the essential factors. Emotional trauma is the experience that distorts the body's movement and form.

The nature of my work is rooted in our sexuality. Very few people want to accept the statement that we are sexual beings, that we are alive in a basically sexual way, and that sexual expression is an indicator of our emotional level of functioning. People are willing to make all kinds of other statements: we are religious beings with a sexual function; we are political-economic beings with a sexual function; we are value-creating organisms that have a sexual part. The thinking can be elaborate, intricate and sometimes quite beautiful, but from my point of view it avoids that truth: that fundamentally we are sexual beings, and we live sexual lives on one level or another. And to the degree that our sexuality is not lived, we are less than we can be.

All the attempts to complicate what we are, are

apologies for the denial of the body, the same denial that has been going on throughout the history of the Christian era.

To affirm that *you are your body*, which is a sexual embodiment, is a great taboo. The acceptance of that statement puts a stop to fantasies, to ideals and illusions about a spiritual life separate from the living body. It brings us to the fact of our dying, of accepting the body's urges to deal with *this* life.

It undercuts in one shot all the rationale, all the justification for the body-hating philosophies in our culture: the acceptance of making the body suffer, of making it a victim, the doing of self-sacrificing deeds which continually deny one's own body for higher principles. To affirm our bodies makes our biological process a personal and a communal ethic.

Affirmation of your embodiedness does *not* require denial of the fact that life is the creator of us all, that we are life, and that dying brings us again to the pool of universal, non-personal existence.

I see the business of living as being the unique processes that express themselves in the continuousness of the life of the body. These life dynamics leave the door open for the parapsychological and religious experience. We have been deeply conditioned to spiritualize, to abstract the body's energies, to consider being evolved, mature, really human separately from corporeal existence. We have been taught to futurize, to moralize, to escape the desires of the flesh, to manipulate our sexuality and dread our bodiliness. This created fantasy became the worlds inhabited and dealt with as if they were the primary truths. We exist in our brains, to keep us alienated from the experience of our bodiliness. To be fascinated by the world of the mind is to be unable to live the body's destiny, to be unable to exist freely.

If we grasped the truth that we are our bodies, we would not tolerate the emotional tortures that we inflict upon ourselves individually and collectively, that twist and deaden our bodies, or that addict us to stimulation. Nor would we bear the body-crippling environment that our culture is creating. If we really experienced what we are doing to our bodied selves, we would rise up and alter the situation to bring it more into harmony with our biological needs. We bear these crimes against ourselves by denying the life of the body, and think of ourselves as worn out or defective machines.

Today theologians, educators, politicians and scientists are saying that we are living at the abyss, that our existential moment is the core of nothingness, empty, that we are a culture without an initiatory rite or a future, that God is dead. I would translate "God is dead" as our bodies are dead, as is our belief and trust in the feelings of our bodies. This has created an emotional, spiritual desert, the destruction of the world of our past, and a future that praises reason so highly that we are without emotional roots.

Our dislike of our biological selves has birthed an initiation that is probably the most sophisticated, elaborate and successful initiatory rite in human history. We initiate in the way we treat the birth process, the way we treat infants, the way we educate children and adolescents. The interrupting of body contact between mother and child at birth, the warnings against breast feeding, and the imposing of early toilet training are all well-implanted stages of our initiatory rite. Our system of education crowds out the instinctual pleasures of life and promises substitute pleasures: mental rewards.

The hatred of sexuality, the fear of sex is succinctly expressed in Robert Graves' *The White Goddess*, when he says that the early Christians so disliked sexuality and the tie to it, they claimed that if humans would stop copulating, a crisis of life's ongoingness would occur, God would be forced to intervene, and there would be salvation from our biological lives.

Our Bodies

I'M COMMITTED TO STUDYING the life of the body through its energetic process, which I understand to be a kind of exciting bio-electrical process. The body is a bio-electric ocean, an excitatory ocean whose currents form both our bodies and our interactions. Just as we understand the universe by its energetic process, in the sun and in the stars, so I try to understand the human personality as the energetic processes of the body, the qualities and quantities of excitement and movement which sustain the living, bringing satisfaction and pleasure.

You are your energy. Your body is your energy. The unfolding, the development of your biological process is you, is you as body. Your body is an energetic process, going by your name.

It's a concept of rich promise. It delights me to say that I am my body, with deep understanding of what that means, as I experience my bio-electrical currents. It gives me identity with my aliveness, without any need to split myself, body and mind. I see all my process—thinking, feeling, acting, imaging—as part of my biological reality, rooted in the universe.

Anything that interferes with this diminishes our connection with ourselves and everything around us. We take a contracted stance in the world without even knowing it, primarily by contracting our body's muscles. When our energy flow of feeling is chronically insulted, our contractedness becomes the way in which we express ourselves, with limited aliveness.

Chronic muscular contractions have functional and emotional consequences. We have two legs and two arms as extensions of our torso. The legs are on the ground; they walk and maintain stability, give us a feeling of sureness, and trust to walk and run—that's their business. They ground us. The arms are different organs of contact. They grasp the world, reach out, manipulate and touch, extend us to others. Anything that inhibits the flow of sensation or the expression of energy in these organs immediately disrupts our connectedness, our pleasurableness, our effectiveness. Muscular contractions say how we are in the world, how we function and respond.

We humans have a magnificent form, and have developed the most expressive range of movement of any animal on earth. That's a crucial truth. It underlies our unique ability to feel and form our lives in indi-

vidualistic ways. When our range of movement expands, our vitality for living, for satisfaction, increases. Yet most of us choose to remain in the program of our chronic contractions.

We choose our imprisonment. This paradox is
dramatized in *A Man for All Seasons*. When Sir Thomas
More refuses to give a divorce to the king, he's torn
between his freedom of movement and his religious
and political duties. His inner dialogue goes like this:
"As long as I behave properly, I am safe; I can think
whatever I want and I am safe within the catacomb of
my mind. I need only allow my outward behavior to be
proper and I can think whatever I want." More's
dilemma is a perfect example of how one chooses
supremacy of mind over freedom of organismic
movement. Suppress movement to stay alive. Im-
prison the body to liberate the mind. That's where we
are now. "Sit still in the classroom, kids, while we
drum knowledge into your heads." "Control your
movement while you're making love. If you don't,
you'll feel impotent." "Power is more important than
contact."

There are people who ask "What the hell are we
alive for? What am I alive for?" They are evidently not
feeling their bodies. The desperation doesn't come
from a decaying of values; it comes from the fact that
the body is no longer vital and pulsatory.

We are told how to be, not just allowed to express
ourselves. And although the body survives these inhibiting rules, it shows that it hasn't lived its own life.
Our cells never get a chance to mature.

My work is to excite the body, to help ignite the metabolic fire. I'm not working to resensitize people, to get them more in touch with their senses, but to be responsive. Excitement is the binding substance of life, the substance of love. When you begin to experience this, to feel it and let it be called out of you—literally evoking life—you begin to be erotic.

I don't see what I do as therapy. I dislike the idea of fixing which the word "therapy" suggests. It does not communicate what happens between me and people I work with. The words grounding, opening, and participating, connecting vital responsiveness, seem appropriate.

Gracefulness
and Streaming

I DEFINE HEALTH as gracefulness. A graceful person is a healthy person.

Every organism has a unique pattern of movement. That pattern of movement is graceful because it is an expression of its natural self, its innate self. It has its own authority, its own truth. Everyone can see it. The gracefulness is an intactness that expresses the being of the creature.

The minute there is a restriction—"Don't," "Don't reach for the breast," "Don't defecate; it's shameful," "Don't make too much contact with me because I can't bear it"—the organism must contract. The contracting breaks the flow from feeling to expression. We become awkward, out of grace.

The act of contracting limits both our movement

28

and our perceptual possibilities. This contraction is our *history* of a particular event. If the event is repeated and the contraction becomes chronic, this basically contracted state programs our philosophy of who and what we are. In a very literal way, it is our form, and our form in turn dictates our expression.

Every chronic contraction prevents the spontaneous and the mysterious, the perceptions and expressions of you. Every prolonged contraction diminishes feeling in your body. Every deep contraction blocks you from your own deep rhythms, with which you are renewed.

The fundamental state of aliveness is a *streaming* state. Few people know from their personal experience what I mean by streaming, for few of us have this contact with ourselves. Yet streaming is a basic cellular function. If you have seen protoplasm through a microscope, you will see that it streams, it has currents, it flows.

Energy flow develops from a state of vibratory excitement, to a pulsatory state, to a state of rhythmic streamings. This continuum of energetic development is what the organism experiences and feels. And these are the states I work for: these qualities of plasmatic mobility that the tissue is able to manufacture for itself. They are states of life. And the more they ripen, the more you are yourself and the world.

Diminishing our connection with these basic biological states produces shame, guilt, anxiety, feelings of alienation. Our reality is experienced as a loss of contact, a deadening—a disconnectedness.

For me, the ability to pulsate, to vibrate, to allow feeling to build up from that fundamental level and determine contact, is the same as the feeling described in our culture as love.

If you follow this thinking further, you'll see that there can be a kind of aging which we could call a rich maturity. Biologically, the tissue of a mature organism is deeply imbedded and expanded contactfully into its environment. A mature tree is gnarled, strong, and beautifully graceful. There is a quality of experience written into it that you can see. It is not withered and dried up; the life is not gone. Animals that have not been too domesticated are vital according to their ages. When their time comes to die, they die very quickly. Their life stream simply runs out. For most of us poor humans though—contracted and repressed—life never has a chance to gracefully develop and deepen contact and connectedness. Instead we battle against life, trained and tabooed, twisted, pained, so that death comes as a shattering collapse rather than as a final fulfillment of life's course.

Deep chronic contractions prevent true aging, which is really maturing. Maturing is a deepening contact with life, and the ability to sustain and refine that contact. It does not have to be the shrinking life space that is usually described as old age and is the result of our self-corseting.

Evolving Sexuality

WHEN WE SOFTEN our fears, our sensuality becomes available to us. We move toward being more sensually and genitally sexual. This growing sexuality and sensuality is our groundedness. Fear of this weakens our connection with self and others. We cut ourselves off from joyful, spontaneous, non-servicing, non-performing sexuality. Instead, we live with concepts and performances.

Being more alive means being more sexual, more sensuous. To be more sexual is to broaden one's range of feeling and expressive action. Most of us try to discover the secret of life, or a greater appreciation for life, in terms of the mind. The first step, however, is to the basic excitement whose patterns of expression create the experiences, urges and images that enrich our minds. That's why I use active techniques in my work. People mobilize excitement through movement and breathing, and express their feelings as they evolve them.

We learn to deal with excitement as we generate it, and this is how personality develops. I use approaches that facilitate the movement of excitement rather than controlling movement. And I use breathing to increase feeling. There is little aliveness without good breathing. Breathing is more than a mechanical event; if we confine our understanding to the mechanical level we don't begin to understand what breathing is in relation to feeling. Life includes the mechanical but is not mechanistic. We too often exaggerate our mechanical understanding and turn our universe into a machine, as Newton did. But this is nonsense. The universe and our bodies are not machines.

Our movement has contraction and expansion phases. This motion creates ourselves and our world. Chronic muscular contraction inhibits this pulsation. Every muscular contraction presents an attitude, a life experience, a way of existing which negates other possibilities of existing. At the opposite end of the spectrum, every overexpansion which prevents boundaries from forming is also negating existential possibilities.

Muscular contractions are not isolated events. They also involve the brain and encompass whole segments of the body, whole functional areas. They come about in different ways. Let's take toilet training, a deliberately imposed social requirement which largely ignores the healthful way in which the body evolves. We ask a child, whose nervous and muscular systems are not ready for voluntary control, to begin to control himself. Now what is that child supposed to do? How is he supposed to do this?

The child finds a way by creating contractions with those muscles that he does have some control over. In doing this, he learns something nonverbally. This learning may not be good for him except in terms of the social rewards he gets. He'll have no idea of how he made it come about. But what he has done restricts his movement and interferes with his range of expression. Worst of all, incorporating the compulsive behavior patterns, the continual muscular contraction, which may protect him from the shame learned around bowel functions, also interferes with the muscles of walking and standing, and with copulating movements. The knees and hips don't easily bend, the buttocks don't move. Loving, walking and standing no longer occur easily and feelingly. The contraction prohibits it, inhibits pleasure, and he walks around unsatisfied and doesn't know why.

The current emphasis is on reawakening just the senses and calling that sensuality. Sensuality does not consist in being more able to use your hands, or in developing your sense of touch. I don't believe that what we are working with is rooted in the sensory apparatus, even though this apparatus is part of it. We're working with deep biological processes that antedate the sensory system.

Your inner ocean is sensual. Your blood and your other body fluids possess a quality of sensuality which moves you from the inside, bathing you. To experience it is to know what I'm talking about.

Sensuality matures, evolves, one of its signs being breathing that extends from the pelvis and genitals to the crown of the head, sending sensation flooding through the whole of you, connecting and unifying you. If you curtail this flow of your excitation, limiting your sensuality, you attenuate your bodiliness, your groundedness.

When making love, you're aware of your excitement, but you can also be aware of an oceanic feeling that makes our sexuality, our bodiliness global, that connects us in a non-conceptual, loving way. That's what we bring to life and receive from life. The social rules that dictate how we are supposed to act in a production-oriented world don't permit that quality of being alive.

I'm not postulating some totally unconscious, hedonistic state. I feel that a person who is feelingly alive is a reality-oriented person who is able to work. I think such a person who is alive is a creative person. And in living this kind of aliveness he doesn't have to do anything: he doesn't have to be unusual; he doesn't have to create unusual things or situations; he doesn't have to create novelties—he simply reveals the universalities of being alive.

I'm talking about bringing ourselves back to our basic oceanic feeling, the basic sensuality of our excitory continuum. We can't seem to accept our common aliveness, and that's a real problem. We can't accept this very basic fact which unites our world. We all have this aliveness in common. This is how we are connected; this is the fundamental existence we share.

A person is not in or out of *touch* with his body. He *is* his body. We need to get rid of this crazy idea, "I have a body." It's the other way around. This is a fact we may not want to swallow, but the head is not the chief cook and bottle washer; the whole body is.

Everybody is seeking aliveness, everybody wants to be more alive. What we don't consider is that we have to grow accustomed to being more alive, to assimilating the energetic charge that flows through each of our bodies. We teach ourselves how to let the charge from our genitals and our respiration really sink in and saturate our tissues, so that our head connects with its own source.

This is the ground that I have been referring to, the ground of experience. If you're an alive body, no one can tell you how to experience the world. And no one can tell you what truth is, because you experience it for yourself. The body does not lie.

Excitation
and Feeling

FROM THE TIME that a person recognizes wanting a person of the opposite sex, the drive to enter or be entered increases. How much foreplay is wanted is each person's business; but there is always pressure toward a forward-going entry. The desire to reach out, fuse, interlock is what overcomes distance; it's the bridge between the man and the woman. The woman is wanting, with her own assertively reaching hips, and rhythms. The man and woman work toward combined rhythms of interpenetration.

Overcoming distance is the function of the swelling penis, the swelling vulva. The partners move toward each other, and a certain amount of resistance heightens the excitation. They may want to kiss and bite and hold, but they're under the impulse to connect.

If a person is living a sexual life and living out of his sexual feeling, then a lot of life is foreplay. Heightened and exaggerated foreplay is a compensation for what's missing from the rest of life. If the life is anchored in sexuality, then sex is not a bedroom matter only. Foreplay is already part of the life expression.

It is possible to live a sensual life if this is what we choose. Most of us don't; we don't even know about it. All people are capable of this kind of life, so it's a matter of lousy education or, more accurately, a matter of an education designed to serve the needs of an industrial, performance-oriented culture. As long as the man cannot share his fullness, he must turn into a work-productive organism. And the woman is taught to be dependent upon the man's assertiveness, his rhythms and schedules.

So limited sexuality is built right into our culture. The first thing that happens to a child is that the breast is not given at all or taken away too early. This dampens sexuality immediately; it cuts off sensual contact. So does discouraging bodily contact, and teaching alienation. Later comes our idealization of marriage. We create a set of rules for sexuality that is unrelated to the pleasure of the activity. Take a look at a book called *The Cradle of Erotica,* by R.E. Masters. You'll begin to see the kinds of sexuality that are encouraged in the mid-Eastern world, and how we've rejected it and developed a "civilized," spiritualized, legalized sex-negative code.

In our culture, the reward is always something

you can have after you have fulfilled a certain task. That's the bait! Pleasure comes *after* work; there is to be no pleasure in the work itself. It may be good to work, but pleasurable—no.

We live on the assumption that we will find rewards and peace in the fruits of our labor, like money, and in the future or in the next world. This philosophy is inherent in every single education program, in every religious program, and in nearly every home. "Reward is in the future," and it is of the mind, or of some deed, not of feeling or desire. This is what we teach.

We can see how sex-negative attitudes get structured in the body by looking at the example of a male homosexual I had as a client. His body and personality were characterized by very deep contractions at the root of the penis and in the whole pelvic section. He experienced that his penis was removed from his body, outside his body. In talking with homosexuals, I hear that sexual excitement is something to be gotten rid of. "I have so much sensation that I've just got to relieve myself of it." The homosexual experiences *peripheral* excitement. His excitation is rarely pleasurable feeling; it is relief, but not satisfaction.

In the clitoral character, the female counterpart to the male homosexual, there is hyperstimulation of the clitoris without an inward deepening of feeling. This, produces a high level of excitation, stimulation with either increased physical or fantasy activity without conversion into feelings. Then the woman confuses excitation with feeling.

As we move toward sexual maturity, hyped-up

sexual excitation becomes secondary, and the quality of our feelings determine sexual identity. That's the difference between adolescent and adult sexuality. What we see around us is a great deal of fantasy stimulation to make us feel excited. We have manipulated ourselves into accepting stimulation rather than feeling. We've done this by sacrificing our bodies as the sources of our feelings of aliveness, and becoming addicted to the brain and nerves as the pleasure center.

I differentiate between four orgastic states: two for the men, two for the women. From the woman's point of view there's the clitoral orgasm and the uterine orgasm. For the man, there's the tip-of-the-penis experience, which is the homologue of clitoral expression, and then there's the more global experience which he feels starting from high up in the region of the solar plexus.

There is a great difference between how the body responds to peripheral arousal and how the body responds to a more internalized arousal. For both the man and the woman, the internalized experience depends upon a commitment to one's feelings and needs, as well as to another person, whereas the clitoral or end-of-penis experience expresses limited commitment. Half the problem of so-called frigidity is that most people are not really willing to deal with their own limited notions of freedom and commitment. They'd rather make frigidity their problem, or not having a satisfactory orgasm, or whatever.

Loving allows that which is unknown to become

known. The unpredictable, unprogrammed feelings and movements are allowed to surface. And this emerges to the same degree that we are willing to give commitment to its emerging. I want to bring that home because it's a very practical statement. The problem is not how you take care of hidden tensions. It is how you choose to deepen your experience.

For many of us, because we have not eroticized our world, sexuality has become the relief of a need, the release of a cramp, the surrender to a compulsion.

Children's masturbation is usually episodic and secretive. Masturbation serves to give children a sense of their own power and independence. However, if carried on into adulthood, to compensate for contact and touch deprivation it serves to further alienate us, and diminish our social power. Masturbation, like peripheral stimulation, gives a particular quality to the soup of our sexuality. It generates a continuum of sensations which is very different from a continuum of feeling. As a man, I would rather be with a woman from the experience in which our feelings and movements developed rhythmically toward climax, than structure my life on the sensations of a fantasy.

The sexual feelings which arise like a pervasive musk from the well of our bodily processes have always been known to be qualitatively different than the sensations aroused by titilation. There's no aphrodisiac that substitutes for the arousal of natural desire.

Families and societies that accept their flesh and blood generate the feelings of sexuality that connect us in an organic way. Families and societies that deny or denigrate the body need to stimulate sexuality through propaganda and advertisements, either to relieve depression or flagellate us into activity.

The Family
Is a Living Body

THE FAMILY IS A LIVING BODY. It is the incubator and channeller of excitement and feeling. It is survival and sexually oriented. Streamers of excitement connect the family members as they breathe together in a common ocean of blood and place. The family—whether of traditional structure: father, mother and children; or of an extended kind: many mothers and fathers and uncles; or just a couple—is a living organism. We cannot live alone. We cannot survive and take care of our needs alone. We cannot even love alone. We humans desire others. We crave company, we gather in bands. Only the mythic hero does without others, cuts himself off from family.

The mother-child bodily interaction, and then the family's physicality, are the bases for how we use our own bodies and how we interact physically with others. How the family relates to being touched by the stimuli of the world of nature makes the world concrete and cohesive. The patterns of behavior, our physicality given us by our families, are meant to ensure survival through proper action with others and in obtaining food and shelter. Families teach about the public world, but present-day families leave us destitute about how to live with our private bodies.

Our life in the womb—with its pulsating fluids and flesh, its rhythms of blood and breath—is meant to be continued after birth in the closeness of skin contact, skin touching as in breast feeding, in being held and carressed, pressed to the warm body of the mother, and of the family, and in sharing sleeping space and bathing. This continuum of contact—the rhythms, the river of breathing with its sounds, the stimulation of the senses of sight, sound and smell, the taste of others' bodies, their pressure and heat as well as their gestures and expressions—is the ocean of our environment outside the womb. The ocean's solids, liquids, gasses form electric currents that filter through membranes, nourishing living. Sensations and feelings also pass through membranes, connecting the social world with the cellular existence.

This ocean is spread thin when we do not encourage bodily contact, holding, touching, rocking and playing, breast feeding; when we breast feed dressed so that the child's lips touch only the nipple, when we isolate children in separate rooms, or when we bathe them alone. Sleeping, bathing, playing, working together, touching and emoting sustain the interacting currents of feeling that organize our space and time, our existence. This strongly interactive kind of contact keeps people and objects close, does away with the feeling of alienation and the sense that the world is alien and out there.

To reach out, to touch, overcomes distance. To push away, expel, creates distance. To taste, to smell, to hold creates familiarity. To sustain our ocean, our atmosphere of living, creates our connection to others, our universe. To touch ourselves and others incites the imagination. To be held with fear, at a distance, to be forced to withdraw, makes the world unfamiliar, fearful, sterile.

Excitement, pleasure and satisfaction connect the bodies that have played and worked together. Pleasurable bodily experiences humanize us, they communicate bodily messages that extend our social actions, our interactions with other human beings. This social outreaching encourages the development of active and receptive contact, the willingness to be aroused and to arouse. Think of animals grooming each other, playing with each other, hunting together, foraging together.

The maintaining of family or clan closeness, the encouragement of skin and feeling contact, does not have to be carried to the extreme where one's privacy is undermined or destroyed—just as the telling of dreams or fears to one's family does not make the whole of one's psyche public. The loss of family bodiliness, in fact, results in the need for group nudity and exhibitionism, the curiosity to see and the urge to be seen, as well as leading to the excessive fear of exposure. The hunger to be touched and to touch drives many people to see doctors and to dream up injuries for physiotherapists. The inhibited need to cry results in the formation of substitute crying, like complaining.

The natural consequence of closeness is the desire for distance, just as distance craves closeness. Contact is pulsatory: it contracts and expands. Feeling has its curve of up and down. Having physical and psychological contact available gives us the option to form our own pattern of privacy instead of being driven to a person. The way we teach our children to be individuals emotionally and socially is wrong. It's too extreme. The extremeness—the teaching of the ability to bear human distance and to solve problems alone—works, when successful, to produce a people who think only for themselves, not with others or cooperatively. They tend toward being unemotional and unpleasuring, reasoners and loners. Being alone, standing in one's crib wailing for contact without a response from another, certainly increases one's feeling of oneself. But it's a cold self-reliance. A friend gave me this clipping:

> "Solitary trees if they grow at all grow strong; and a boy deprived of a father's care often develops, if he escapes the period of youth, an independence and vigour of thought which may restore in after life the heavy loss of early days." *The River War*
> Winston Churchill

When it fails, we see the type of dependency and

unsureness that turns people into followers. We see crippling through excessive need for contact and approval, inability and unwillingness to act alone or differently.

Ashley Montagu says touching completes the nervous system. I say touching completes the feeling process. The family, the emotional clan or tribe, is our extended uterus. In the Christian world we are linked by ideas, not feeling. That is why Montagu can make the above statement, but I say touching completes the feeling process.

We never outgrow our need for touching and holding. Our skin is an extension of our feelings. The surface of our body teaches our brain about the world. The brain learns from how we respond emotionally. There is an inevitable experience and feeling that results from touch or no-touch—an experience that paints for us a picture of a friendly or unfriendly world. The discouragement of bodily contact, be it the substitution of words for touching or through expressions of dislike, through isolation or making a child be alone too long too early, produces not only intense longing for contact and painful self-experience but feelings of helplessness, shame and self-hate ("I hate myself for wanting," or "I feel shame when I need to be held"). This undermines the bodily self which is the very basis of self-esteem.

There is often a double message in a family. "I love you, I care for you; I just reject the touching of your body. I love you as long as you do not bother me." This stiffens us, leads us to stifle our screams, and makes us subject to unexplained rages. Our body rejection is the betrayal of ourselves.

A family crisis can be defined as an increase in excitation that demands more than the ordinary responses. If this response is forthcoming, the crisis brings emotional and instinctual as well as social satisfaction. In my work with people, trying to undo their inhibitions and taboos, to soften their feelings of somatic rejection, I and others have found that heavy musculature or weak musculature are expressions of the time in our lives that we have met crisis. Deprivation during the first two to three years generally creates underdeveloped muscles and weak skin tone. After that the response to crisis is usually a stiffening of body form or deep withdrawal, like a sunken chest or a pulled-in abdomen. Therefore, when through the psychological/physical process there is an increase in excitement, the fears that emerge are ones of being helpless, not knowing what to do with the excitement or how to respond, fears of the unknown and of punishment. The response can reveal the family history as well as the history of the individual.

We promise our growing young that when they reach the proper age, they can again live in close physical contact with another, that they can sleep together and touch intimately. At the same time, we train the youngsters to be alone, to learn to be lonely and endure it, to do without physical contact, to weaken the bonds of bodily pleasure and to strengthen the bonds of morality. We continually ask children to bear separation, less and less physical touch and shared feeling—and then we want to know why intimacy and trust is disappearing in the family, why the family is breaking down. By bodily denial, we preach privacy and shame, forced independence.

The family links the individual to its past and future through the preservation of myth and the transmission of experience. Experiencing an atmosphere of mistrust and little intimacy, the child absorbs the myths of fear and aggression. Denied sexual knowing and approval, he learns to distrust his bodily responses and chooses an economic, idealized life.

A person's body reflects the family's history and the values that have been perpetuated. All families form the bodies that express their emotional and moral values. For example, I recall a family that had a strong powerful father, six feet tall, muscular and successful in business, with a strong will and deep religious belief. He had a ramrod spine, was prudish, and was married to a bubbly wife with seductive girl-like behavior. They raised three children, two boys and a girl. The boys, raised for success in the business, failed. One son resisted his father, imitating him with a ramrod spine. He would blanch and fade away when his father was around. He could barely earn a living; his father supported him. His brother, meanwhile, rebelled, responding with a collapsed chest and hunched shoulders to the pressure of his father and the seductive placating of his mother. The girl also had a crushed-in chest and low self-esteem, but a sexy pelvis; she'd been reared to be seductive and submissive. Excitement was not tolerated in this family, only obedience to orders. All had to pay homage to the king, so all had to go out and win, but not to unseat or displease papa in the process.

All people are born with their own rhythmical pulsations, with their own peristaltic movements formed as they leave the birth canal. These peristaltic waves are the movement of life, are in tune with the mother, and are the basis of the child's life as it establishes them in the post-uterine world. These waves reach out toward the mother, to nestle, to suck, etc. Our pulsations are sexual, are the self, are emotional survival.

How the family regulates its life in relation to these rhythms of pulsation and streaming helps determine how the child relates to the family. It writes the rules of this living unit. When the family teaches the child to diminish excitation—to be quiet, reserved, to regulate itself according to the parents and not to affect the vibrations of the others—we see depressiveness, or the weakening of the bonds of bodily contact that inhibit reaching out, that discourage intuitive connections, that encourage placating, submissiveness, resentfulness, dependency. If the rule is to exaggerate the bodily rhythms—if the family pushes the child to be overactive, if they over-demand of it and behave seductively with it, or if they don't interact at all and continually let it have its way—we find defiance, rebellion, blaming, accusing, impulsiveness, self-centeredness.

There is no survival without a family of one sort or another, if not of blood then of emotional bonds. If there is no herding, no group to give emotional contact, support and sharing, we have schizophrenia.

A mother told me that she and her husband had decided to let their six-month old child cry for 10-15 minutes before going to her. I pointed out that this was a way of teaching her to be alone, rather than a way of teaching her to be independent. They were sending her a double message: We love you . . . but stop needing us. Learn to bear the isolation, start tolerating the roots of what we call individuality. Stop needing us as a baby and start growing up.

We deliver this cultural message, and its double bind becomes the core of our family life. This is how we learn to live our civilized life of: be sociable but don't touch, be yourself but please us. The double message at its worst drives us to despair and into schizophrenic states. At best it makes us sensitive to abstractions and to hypocrisy.

We place value on children learning to be able to handle their upsets alone. They learn to be alone by deadening themselves, forming deep chronic muscular contractions. But it rarely works for long. Those who do not succeed live in dread of the desires of the flesh, or shamed by their weak submission to desire. Those who suppress the upsets well live with contempt for their novacained bodies, and contempt for others. When we are bodily awake, and our feelings are not allowed to connect with others, we often develop anxiety, because we want physical contact and others do not.

Feelings and needs find satisfaction—or are

inhibited—through muscular action. The excitement of
hunger or the need to be touched can end in crying or
masturbation, in fights or withdrawal. We can close off
and not pay attention to our crying, or we can protest,
be destructive. In an anti-feeling family situation, we
have to do something to ourselves so that our excitation doesn't hurt. We deaden ourselves, we divert
ourselves. This helps form our family shape.

Children want their parents to respond to them.
Parents respond, on one level, to a child's needs.
They're also responding to something in themselves
that is being aroused by the child. Children say, "I
must make you respond to me," first with crying, then
with screams. And the parents stiffen up to ward off
their own anger or fear, their desire to respond. Deep
down they are having to squeeze their own fear of
being alone. When the child finally gives up, and
either stiffens against its own impulses or collapses,
we have a family body that expresses, "Don't cry,
don't want contact, learn to be alone," represented by
individual bodies that are stiff or collapsed.

Reaching out is one phenomenon, whether in
adults or children. Young children reach out to their
parents, which is their world, and adults reach toward
their world of other adults.

Children's excitation calls out universal mothering
patterns—though there are women who are deeply
inhibited and do not respond as mothers. Later on, as
the child begins to have energy for its own innovative
behavior, it will create situations that demand individual, not archetypal, responses. It will call out some-

thing more than the mothering pattern. The excitatory process will call out something new in the mother and father. In the whole family, something new will be evoked.

Excitation creates muscular action and emotional expression. Looking at somebody's emotional and muscular expression, we can see the body form developed as the child begins to ask his parents to respond to him as an individual person. For example, a woman named Sally whom I worked with told me about her sexual difficulties. She said she gets excited when making love, and then all of a sudden her excitement goes flat. It just dies on her. I pointed out that every time she gets into a confrontation that requires sustained self-assertiveness, she collapses. Her body slumps.

In her youth her excitement met her mother's stony religiousness and her father's playfully sadistic pokes which on a number of occasions did her physical harm. So her every assertive movement is accompanied by a shrinking slump. She sticks out her jaw and her chest collapses. She demands attention and her voice is flat. She raises her fist in anger and her lower body trembles. She gets excited sexually, and she fears to go forward to focus and climax her feeling. Her mother never raised her voice. So when she exercised her own assertiveness, she never evoked response that was affirmative—just disapproval or hurtful criticism. She was never permitted to do things her way. She was always corrected. Or when she reached to her parents with demand or anger, it was deflected by being made fun of or reasoned with. No wonder her excitement went flat.

Sally was encouraged by her father to be excited and punished by her mother for it. She was encouraged to be pleasing and obedient and punished for being assertive. If she was sexual she was disapproved of. Yet her father aroused her, and her mother taught her to please by placating. If she pleased she was dooming herself. Damned if she did and damned if she did not. She couldn't be a woman or a child. The resolution was to be a perpetual girl. This was her slump.

Our family determines how we find our ground, how we form our territory. If we do not have plenty of touching and holding, we may never be sure of ourselves emotionally, of the ground we stand on, since we cannot trust others to hold us. It's been my experience, as well as others', that people who are not held enough have a fear of falling and hold themselves stiffly away from the earth. Those who feel shame for their sexuality and dislike for their bodily responses never really hold their ground with others. They are always proving themselves or shrinking from others. They are weak-kneed. All warm-blooded animals learn to play, learn to be excited and spontaneous, learn to laugh and do the unexpected, to come close and go far away. If our family does not encourage this natural function of contact and withdrawal, we lose the ability to jump, to get off the ground, to hop around. If our family is not comfortable with this we learn their heaviness.

We are conceived by others, we are nurtured by another, we are born with others, we live with others: clan, family, whatever. The consistent history of our lives is this in-touch-ness with others, this skin-to-skin-ness, this contact through sensations, feelings, needs, this connection through gestures and action, smell and sound, vision and vibration that gives rise to the currents of intuition and the waves of excitement that form the group body as well as our bodies. We thrive in this non-verbal continuum, in this world of the family as ourselves.

To be born is to be touched
To die is to be untouched
To touch is to learn
To hold is to behold
To have a family is to be free
To have no family is to search
all of one's life
for what is missing.

THE
HUMAN
GROUND

Being Grounded

THERE IS AN ARTIFICIAL DISTINCTION between mind and body. This separation of thinking and action from feelings, has caused an almost universal distance between us as bodies and what we identify as the self. Yet our feelings, our thoughts and actions are a connected, energetic bodily process.

Similar to the transmission of nerve impulses, breathing also generates a bio-electrical current, and touching generates an emotional current. Human expression heightens and combines electrical and emotional currents. The body is an electrical-emotional field.

Most people don't understand that this bio-electrical and emotional process is generated by cellular activity in the form of desire, a field that thrusts its way toward actions, creating feeling. Desire is the ground of the miracle of living; what we experience emotionally is a bio-electric process. My desire shapes me. Desire is our ground.

All living tissue has in it a circulation. In the molecular world, one sees it as the flow of electrons. In the cellular, it is the flow of protoplasm. On the organismic level it is the circulation of fluids. At all levels, this movement creates shape and connection. This flow is called streamings. In the human realm it rests specifically on need and satisfaction. This is the human ground.

There is that which enhances this energetic streaming and there is that which diminishes it. We can dissipate it or we can focus it. We can let it live in one part of ourselves and deny it in another part of ourselves. Its amplitude and intensity are directly related to our involvement and experience in living.

To experience separation from our streamings causes us to behave as if we were trees uprooted from the earth: we lose connection with our source of nourishment, support, and ability to grow. We lose our groundedness. This loss is expressed in the shape of our body; it affects our uprightness. When we stand, we don't relate well to gravity. Disappointed, disapproved desire diminishes our dignity.

To be grounded is to be connected to our emotional-electrical currents, to the waves of our needs and images and the rhythms of actions which comprise our physical-psychic processes: the rhythms of the human and natural ground.

Grounding roots our needs and desires, connects us to the earth, which transmits its own flow to us in turn. It's an actual process of connection, communication and satisfaction. Stand on one foot; experience your feeling of connection with the ground and its effect on you. Now massage your foot, stand again, and re-experience the connection. This same process goes on between people. Increased contact is increased desire, the enriching of connection as sensation and image.

A person having contact with his own body is in contact with feelings, desires, sensations, and pleasures. At the same time, he feels related to the natural environment of which he is a part. He responds to the content and the interconnectedness of the natural world. When a person is grounded, his experience enables him to understand that he is a somatic process, that he is his flesh and blood.

A person who lives in his images, who denies his body's feelings and needs or tries rigidly to control them in such a way that he rises above them, acts destructively in relation to himself—which can mean anything from flagellation to asceticism to overindulgence. It is commonplace to do something to the body, as if everyone recognizes that the body is the ground of experience. By doing something to it one hopes to tap its energy. But in this way one uses the body instead of living it. One bullies it instead of participating in its processes.

We are animals, human animals. We learn either to participate in our animal ground or to affirm our separation from it. For this purpose we have voluntary muscular and nervous systems that enable us to take something of value from our experience and, from that valuation, to create social behavior.

The organs of choice and freedom are already present when we are infants. At birth our self-regulation begins to emerge, and our extended child-hood allows us to use our brains and muscular systems for experimentation and exploration, to aid in our self-formation and satisfaction. All other mammals deliver young which have a capacity to deal with the world quickly. The comparable human learning period (commonly viewed as a period of dependency) is five to ten times longer. The child appears to have been born deliberately premature, purposely unprepared for the world.

Premature birth puts us into the environment before our patterns have become fixed. This gives us opportunities for behavioral learning through timely, non-stressful situations in which we form our own patterns and learn to ensure survival in a variety of ways. Man is truly a uniquely adaptable creature, capable of changing both himself and his environments.

In the proliferating of his energetic process the child makes more and more contact with himself and his world. When the parent discourages this proliferating and superimposes patterns that represent his own ideals and conveniences, then the child's emerging rhythmicities become disharmonious, often to the extent of disrupting his connections with his ground.

The dynamics of superimposition were clearly experienced and expressed by a man who was in a workshop with me. After we had worked with his breathing for a while, he began to understand how an organism gains awareness of itself as its rhythms are reflected back to it from an outside source. He began to understand that as an infant's rhythms are perceived and fed back by the parents, the infant learns to know itself.

Summarizing his experience, this man wrote that, first of all, he became aware of the correlation between his breathing and the rhythm of his mental life—the rhythm of what he heard in his head. He said that this awareness put him in touch with certain mental distinctions of his which, in turn, gave him to recognize the two poles of his existence: self and mirroring. This latter realization enabled him to see that a child is born as an "it," an impersonal force, and that communication with the it-child is possible only through experiencing the child's rhythms (his breathing, feeding, crying)—by holding the child, changing the child, etc. A mutually synchronized rhythmicity occurs when the rhythms of parent and child reflect back and forth. This reflecting or resonating empowers the child's ego and gives him a sense of belonging in the world. An early sense of connectedness allows for the later emergence of disharmonious rhythms, so that the growth of individuality, which respects each person's boundaries, may take place without alienation.

In the womb, the mirroring of the child's rhythm by his environment is at its peak. As the child is born and as his individuality grows, the mirroring becomes gradually weakened. Rather than reflect back the child's rhythm, the parents resume the asserting of their own rhythms. It is in the process of attempting to adjust his rhythm to that of his world that the child develops the two poles: self and other. Basically, this is how a child develops an awareness of "I," how he comes to know himself.

The same young man went on to write:

> Awareness of "I" develops out of distortions; "I" develops as the result of a person's attempt to restore original oneness. Mental activity is predicated on the original oneness of self and mirror. The I, the center of awareness, moves from self to reflection of self by the world in an effort to restore this oneness, to conciliate differences, to make distinctions disappear. Seen this way, inner life is a dialectical process between self and self-image, trying to move back to an original synthesis or oneness. The more distortions and distinctions between self and mirrored-back-self, the more frantic is the pace of this inner dialectic and the more acute is the feeling of self-consciousness.

I pointed out to him that he saw natural development as a negative process, probably because he had problems in his early contacts with his parents.

Our freedom consists in releasing our energy from a narrow band of self-programs. Our long years of learning and forming enhance our ability to channel our energy through the voluntary neuro-muscular organs, including the brain. These organs permit us to unfold and to express our capacity for selection and differentiation—not only in our inner lives (imaginings, dreams, sexual drives, conceptual associations) but also in the converting of our internal life into the public realm as unique social behavior. We do not live by bread alone. We must also satisfy our visions.

One time I was moving my shoulders, and I got more movement than usual in one shoulder by moving the arm in a certain way. The increased movement in that shoulder increased the stimulation to my brain. I was able to feel the difference between one shoulder and the other. I experienced more mobility in my body, which, coupled with the heightened self-perception induced by this mobility, opened my field of choice.

This one small experience is representative of the whole growth process. The expressive movements that we have learned for survival and for pleasure, over millions of years and during the interactive course of each lifetime, constitute the nature of our grounding and the nature of what we transmit to our offspring, by word and by example.

The principal difference between us and our fellow animals is our potential for deepening and intensifying that which arises from our living: the feelings, the inner movements, and the desires that give us the ability to experience and understand in a more and more profound way the meaningfulness and the joy of our being alive. Of course, if we use our voluntary organs to inhibit or over-control this potential for experimentation, the result is diminished aliveness, diminished motility, and the impoverishment of our emotions and sensations. Misuse of, and interference with, our essential natures grows us into our common ailments: fearfulness, rage, confusion, doubt, frustration, and dissatisfied separation from our bodily ground—leading to anguish and despair rather than to a fulfilling of the great possibility for vitality and love with which we have been endowed.

The human animal is an energetic process. We are each of us a process that creates, replicates, maintains, transforms, and generates energy, which is manifested as desire, feelings, images, symbols, gestures, and satisfaction. There seem to be three stages in this process:

a. Vibration. A resonating pattern, much like that obtained by throwing a stone into water or striking a tuning fork. The pattern of excitement forms a field of action, a continuum of oscillating excitation which transmits information that sustains organization. All cells and organs display this.

b. Pulsation. The in-and-out of expansion and contraction, enhanced excitation and diminished excitation, inhalation and exhalation, intensification and relaxation, the buildup of hunger and its satisfaction, the waxing and waning of desire. All of these have crests and troughs. Rhythms are the rates and amplitudes of pulsation, its speed and intensity of replication returning, just as in the tides. One's rhythm of in-and-out is the basis for self-regulation, in sleeping and wakefulness, in hunger of all kinds.

c. Streaming. The energetic patterns of rhythmic pulsation, on a higher level of organization, exhibit a tendency to constant reorganization that appears as a flow. The pulsating continuousness of an organized electrical current tends toward elongation and extension, and density and compression. This process of constant reorganization sweeps the body on the long axis, head to toe and toe to head, whether the body is horizontal or vertical. But with the body in a vertical position, the intensity of the streamings is increased. Increase in intensity generates more focus and feeling.

Streaming is action. It is the organization of desire throughout the body. The expression of energy in the forms of need and action embeds the body in the world. Any interference with this flow provokes rage, anxiety, doubt, weakening of identity or its opposite: self-diminution, helplessness, and depression, or tenacity, adventurousness and hope.

Our bodies are a generating bio-electric ocean, which is manifested, as I said, as needs and feelings, sensations and intuitions, images and actions. This process also develops the membranes by which it contains itself, thereby giving us our shape. Just as the heart contains the blood that fills it, we can let our desires well-up and deepen. The art of self-containment creates self-awareness.

Containment is the means whereby the electrical-emotional current intensifies feelings and sensations, self-perceptions and world-perceptions. Containment comes about in the process of setting up and maintaining boundaries. It includes self-collecting, self-regulating, and the forming of structures for knowing the world. The tissues of the body swell and make pools of feeling which act as visceral "brains." These unacted out desires, with their contained feelings and their non-symbolic mental counterparts (intuitions) reveal the living experience. Containment should not be confused with grasping and contracting, the images of possessiveness and apprehending.

The functions of containing and expressing energy enable us to accomplish the two dimensions of grounding: (1) connecting with the earth, and (2) expanding into the social world. It is through these functions that the child roots himself and forms the bridges from the infantile and adult environments. Interference with one's rooting and expanding is manifested in how one relates to the earth, reflected as poor bodily form, and in how one relates to one's social surround, reflected as misshapen connections with others. But if we are encouraged to develop our groundedness, we generate excitement which yields depth of feeling and imagination, visions from which we can ground our lives.

Shaping the Ground

OUR GROUNDING is a developmental process. Our maturity consists in the ripening tone and quality of our tissues and its emotional and muscular coordination. Our biological maturity can be seen in terms of tissue excitability and tissue motility—how the tissues are able to contain and express their urges. Everybody can tell the difference between the way a baby's body feels and the way an adult's body feels. And everybody knows that most men try to harden their bodies in order to inhibit their feelings. In the western world we have emphasized a maturity of thinking and acting while allowing the infantilization of our feelings.

Maturity is not the same as old age. Old age is a sickness brought about by misusing ourselves. Our maturity is our ability to take and to give, to take in and to extend, to hold back and to express with minimal pre-conditioning. It's our capacity for sustaining what goes through us: our thoughts and images, our emotional tones, etc. It's our willingness to permit events to reveal themselves, to be who we are and to respect our limitations. In our maturity we build up our excitation, intensify it through containment, so that we can shape the situation. We contain a multiplicity of events, let them cook, and unify them into a coordinated expression.

Maturity depends upon tissue motility. Look at two dogs, one of which has been abused and the other loved. Their is a qualitative difference in the juiciness of their flesh. If the cells are contracted and tight, responsiveness to the river of feelings is not supported by tissue tone.

Maturation of tissue is disturbed by chronic attitudes, chronic muscular contractions which limit the development of the flow of excitation—keeping it infantile or rigidifying it. I look for places of the body which are underdeveloped, places which indicate fragmentation or diminution of inner and outer movement.

Infantilism is prevalent in our culture because we rarely interact emotionally, or even bodily. The ability to respond emotionally and to develop a deeper and wider continuum of feelings depends on tissue receptivity and the coordination of neuro-muscular expression. Brain/muscle tightnesses arrest and impede our emotional maturation by interfering with the metabolism of feeling. They bank our cellular fires, dam up our emotional-electrical currents. And it works the other way around: emotional injuries manifest as distortions, twists of the body's muscles and brain.

We use our muscles to satisfy our needs. We operate according to a gridwork of patterns which organize our movements into social action. Overusing a small group of these patterns leaves us poorly grounded. We have taught ourselves certain patterned responses to prevent specific movements. For instance, we have learned not to touch ourselves in the region of our genitals. This gradually comes to feel "natural."

We may inhibit our grounding because we fear pleasure, or because we're afraid that we'll be ridiculed or exploited when our excitement shows. We may inhibit our grounding because we don't know how to deal with change, with new experiences. Our groundedness returns to us when we learn to relax control, when we learn to participate with our own processes and those of others.

Since physical and psychological attitudes are two aspects of ourselves, contraction or its lack tells something about a psychological limitation, and vice-versa. Both tell something about how the person in question is grounded.

To clarify how attitudes determine people's relationships with their ground, I've categorized several responses to a grounding exercise that I use sometimes in workshops. This simple exercise, which consists of hopping on one foot and then standing again with both feet planted, serves to intensify feelings. The interaction between feet and earth communicates information throughout the whole body, and the whole body responds to the extent of this relationship, giving rise to self-knowledge.

Some responses to the exercise indicated an attitude of waiting, which is one way to diminish groundedness:

> I wait to be excited. I get pleasure in letting you do it, and double pleasure when you give it to me of your own free will.

> There is a pushing inside me. The front of my body is tense. My arms are tense. I feel that I'll collapse. I feel a sulking, a reserve. I am always unsatisfied.

> I am cautiously nibbling at life. I never feel sure of the ground. I slouch with my chest sucked in.

> Waiting perpetuates my sense of injustice. It gives me a sense of power, too, and yet I continually feel unloved.

There were a number of responses that came from attitudes of wanting to please:

> I want to please you. I want to show you how bright I am, how good I am. I feel important by making you feel important, and by making you notice me. I do this by keeping busy.

> I am grounded in your approval. I perform a lot.

> I like to excite you because I want attention. But when I get it I get scared and I close down.

> If there weren't all those goals out there I would be afraid. I'd be on my own, and I wouldn't like that at all. Achieving goals makes me feel important, but to achieve I have to hold myself aloof.

I tighten my jaw, pull back in my throat and smile.
I stiffen my spine, pull up the arches in my feet, and
lock my knees. I float on the ground, ready to escape if
need be.

When I feel my legs I feel a brooding anger, and
this feeling frightens me because it makes me want to
say "no" to others, to refuse them. To accept my
ground would mean that I'd be alone.

Finally, there were several attitudes that had to do
with being a helper:

I try to help people. When I do, I stiffen my neck
and my legs. I hunch my back and encourage people
to lean on me. I seek them out. I hold on to others
because I feel empty in myself. I waddle with my head
jutting forward. I like to rescue people in need even
though I feel some grimness and bitterness in me
when I rescue them.

In order to help people I have to plant my self in
my feet, and this makes me feel solid. There's a lot of
pleasure for me in this.

I feel that the essence of me is to change things. So
I like to struggle. This gives me feelings of doing
something. By contrast, I hardly ever feel sexual.

Even more generally, a poorly ungrounded state
leads to physical and psychological attitudes of doubt.
Doubt is a feeling of caution, with images of catas-
trophe. It provokes investigation which tends to defer
action. It is the feeling associated with distrust of one's
own responses, one's own body.

When the circulation of our excitement is constantly tampered with, this provokes doubt, putting us
on guard against being hurt or rejected. Our structures
can be so ridden by doubt, so hesitant and shaky that

we project our feelings onto the world, which then becomes a very unsure place for us.

Interference with our groundedness provokes feelings of worthlessness. This results in our continually needing to prove that we are right, that we are worth something. Worthlessness makes us be grounded in a shrinking way, or we compensate with combativeness in which we are grounded with a stiffness that prepares us, we think, for flight or fight. Or we resist compliance by digging in and being planted. But proving ourselves by imitating others or by being daring, even though it may elicit esteem, leaves us unconvinced of our self-worth at heart.

The organization of energy creates a continuum. A continuum of energetic events is called behavior. A person with a low vibratory or pulsatory rate has less energy and organizes his behavior differently from a person with a higher pulsatory rate. His behavior reflects the way in which his body is organized. In a tight, hard body or in a weak body the excitation is kept low. In a more flexible, more motile person the excitation is higher. In both cases the person's body reveals how he is grounded, how he experiences himself, and how he connects with other bodies.

Increased excitation is perceived as an urge to organize feeling into action. Our excitement has two roots. One is internal, an increase of our cellular metabolism which, through its expansion, presses for expression. The other is external, a charge of information from outside that we receive and respond to. The first is the result of our own process. The second results from someone or something stirring us up.

Action, which can either intensify our excitation or inhibit it, is what we are doing. How we do it demonstrates our style of life: expansive, withdrawn, flamboyant, soft, heroic, polite. Our living experience is integrated in our bodily expression, which becomes a quality of tissue, a quality of structure as well as a quality of thinking and contacting and behaving. It is our self-continuity.

Our actions are muscular and can be identified either with our individual selves or with the culture. We can turn our muscle/brain organ against our instinctual self, restricting our innate desires and replacing them with cultural goals. Yet our muscles are also the organ of self-correction. If we hold our chest high to avoid feeling small, our first job is to undo this holding action. To destructure the contraction, the old way of doing, provides us with excitation that invites or reinstates connection.

Grounding raises trees with roots and branches. Roots establish a ground, a stance, a stance based on self-trust that affirms one's subjectivity, with branches that contact and connect with the social world.

We disrupt our energy flow by creating contractions in our muscular systems and in our organ systems, spasms that inhibit our normal flow of bodily excitation. Chronic contractions disturb our relationships to space, time, and gravity. They interfere with our ability to contain, form, and exchange energies with environment, family, and community.

When we examine a contraction and its emotional

accompaniment we see that psychological and bodily qualities are both manifestations of the same energetic phenomenon. With this insight we can begin to discern a few of the different kinds of diminished groundedness.

If you look closely at people you will notice that the body has some segments that have been used more than others. With some, the head seems mature (shows the experience of exposure to living) while the torso seems immature, held in, and the legs are drawn up tightly as if they have never unfolded. You might see this configuration in someone whose job involves contact with the public. The hands and face permit all the subtleties of aggravation and joy that come from this public contact. The forehead, the eyes, the lips, the cheeks, the fingers have on them the marks of having lived. They are testimony to a ripened capacity for dealing with internal and external events in these areas.

At the beach, you might see that this same individual is living a discrepancy. The rest of his body might exhibit no sign of the maturity of the hands and face. Everything from the head down may look unused, unbreathed, childlike, naive. Whether flabby or stiff, the torso may have only a small range of expression. Obviously it has experienced neither the contact nor the use that the hands and face have experienced.

What does this mean and how does it happen? We know that the natural development of the child takes him from the curled-up flexion of the infant to the extendedness of erect posture. It's a natural unrolling, a very deep and dynamic learning process. To be able to reach out with one's needs and visions, to extend oneself in space, in time, and with relation to others is the most dramatic adventure of the growing child, and creates an emotional atmosphere that enhances biological connection.

Self-extending takes place in the emotional field shared with the parents; while tied emotionally to his parents, the child learns to establish his center of gravity, gaining self-esteem as his organs of independence start to function.

If I ask a person to extend himself, and this is a person who has not fully assumed uprightness and all that is implied in learning to stand on one's own feet, a temporary openness results which evokes feelings in him—feelings of insecurity or security, weakness or strength. Many people resist experiencing feelings. But, if they allow themselves this experience, sooner or later they reveal specific emotional conflicts. There may have been an overly anxious mother who consciously or unconsciously forced the child to stand on his own feet too early, so that he still feels unsure in relation to gravity; or conversely there may have been a father who, consciously or unconsciously, was overly protective and instilled fears of independence. In either case, not only has a somatic immaturity been produced, but a whole emotional tone of unripenedness: this *is* the individual structure as an adult—and, for example, he literally goes weak in the knees when someone else makes demands. When a person finds ways to loosen his contractions, former relationships with his parents come to light in feelings, dreams, and memories which he can then choose to maintain or to re-form as new behavior.

A contraction expresses the desires of the past in the present. The past gets structured in the body's form and also in the body's range of feeling and movement. For example, one says: I don't dare to feel needy, I don't reach out, I grab instead. When the contraction is loosened, one comes to be in the present with what is unstable and newly emerging. Simultaneously, one may be in the world *with* his past, but not *as* his past. Yet the loosening of a contraction does not reveal hidden abilities that are fully matured. It simply presents the opportunity for us to learn and grow, for new unfolding. There is no instant miracle.

If our relationship with the ground is tenuous, then our instinctual life and our body will also be tenuous. Our connection with the mystery of life will be tenuous. What we didn't know is that this weakened connection is structured somatically.

If we contract ourselves, we contract that which is universal in us. All of us are connected with the universal, first and directly with our mothers, and then with our own bodies, our own earth. For a child, the mother's body is the earth. As we grow and develop, our bodies become our ground, our universality.

Contact and
Withdrawal

EXPANSION AND NORMAL CONTRACTION are basic to the
continuing expression of our biological ground, the
sustaining of our biological existence. By expanding
and contracting we take in oxygen and expel carbon
dioxide; we consume food and water and eliminate
waste materials; our hearts beat with the rhythm of
systole and diastole. Energetically, the human being
compresses excitation to a certain point and then expresses it. The orgastic phenomenon operates similarly: a buildup of excitement and feeling followed by a
focused satisfaction.

People who are chronically contracted disturb
their rhythmic pulse in the physical and psychic
spheres. People who are chronically expanded, who
cannot contain themselves, also disturb their fluctu-

ating rhythms. In both cases, these people impair their capacity for taking in and discharging.

A young man I worked with showed symptoms of chronic expandedness. He had a raised chest and a distended abdomen. His body was loose-jointed, and he couldn't keep from talking loudly, making wild gestures. His breathing was short and rapid. Every time I asked him to be still, to hold back a little bit, he flew into a rage that masked his deeper feelings of worthlessness, which was based on poor muscular coordination and lack of containment.

This man had a mother who wanted him to be what she wanted him to be. She kept hyping him up, invading him with her excitement, and meanwhile every one of his own impulses was "wrong." His unwillingness to contain himself was his ongoing attempt to dispel his mother's influence, to neutralize her invasiveness. He was evasive in order to avoid hitting her.

On the other hand, a young woman I worked with created a discontinuity in herself by contracting her buttocks, her bladder, and her uterus. This gave her the feeling of having two different parts. In the course of our work together we found that she wouldn't cry or experience deep satisfaction. Much of this was directly related to prohibitions against tenderness that she had placed upon herself to win love: daddy's good girl does not cry, or in any way indicate that she is needy. To stay in daddy's favor she learned to suppress her physical and emotional softness. Her contractedness expressed, "I will be strong, not weak."

These two examples show how interference with our rhythms of expanding and contracting debilitates us physically, emotionally, and cognitively. The essence of grounding is to maintain the balance of expansion and contraction. We transfer our bodily reality to our social reality, and vice-versa. A balanced person, a grounded person, forms attitudes that he or she can relax. The person swings between the feelings that come from developing boundaries and the feelings that come from giving up old boundaries. To be grounded is not to procure more and more aliveness. To be grounded simply encourages us to live the rhythm of the aliveness we have.

Expansion connects us to the world by testing our boundaries and skills, and by the projection of our images and feelings on the world, which encourages responsiveness. It is us going public. Healthy withdrawing is self-collecting. It is going deeper into oneself, staying more bounded, keeping one's excitement at home. It is us being private, not autistic or depressed.

In my work I seek to stimulate a continuously reorganizing process of expansion-containment, contraction-expression. One way I do this is to work with the breathing, which is a social act. To cry and to laugh, to smile and to sigh not only are activities of respiration, they are meant to communicate. Breathing must be worked with in its social context. To breathe in is to inspire, to get bigger, to take in, to lift oneself off the ground. To exhale is to give back, to make oneself smaller, to come closer to the ground, to expire. The psyche and the soma, one's social actions are all reflected in how we breathe.

Emotional expression broadens and deepens breathing, permitting fuller emotional and social expression: crying, and laughing, and singing and screaming, verbalizing one's needs, standing on one's feet and being independent, allowing oneself to trust another. When our transition from our image to action is meddled with, or when our social out-reaching is rejected, these insults hamper the diaphragm.

The up-and-down movement of the diaphragm creates sensation and feeling. If we cannot tolerate this, we set up contractions throughout our body that restrict it. Similarly, if we cannot tolerate sensations in the throat, for fear of crying or yelling or asking, we constrict the throat.

I work with people whose breathing is contracted and people whose breathing is over-excited. The breathing of some people is both contracted and overextended at the same time. One man confines his breathing to the lower half of his body; this is borne out by his overcharged sex life and his lack of heartfelt emotion. A woman confines her breathing to her chest; she has an overdeveloped social life and underdeveloped sexuality. Diminished breathing in a particular bodily area indicates a low level of excitement there.

Contracted breathing and over-excited breathing present two extremes. Contracted breathing makes one stiff, dense, over-solid. This inhibits oxygenation, there is a buildup of CO_2, an acid state which gives rise to delusions and fantasy life, as in depressives, certain forms of meditation, and acid takers. Over-breathing makes it difficult for a person to control himself, makes him alkaline and convulsive. Think of mania, hysteria. The person is impulsive and over-reactive. His boundaries are fragile. He has difficulty containing; his shadowy sense of individuality permits him to be overwhelmed by feeling. He may swim in self-indulgent pleasure or terror.

Our activity partakes of the process of expansion and contraction. Expressions generate impressions. We express ourselves by impressing ourselves on the world. The world expresses itself by impressing us. In this exchange, we are ourselves and we become somebody. We ground our bodies, and we shape our common ground, the earth.

Sex and Love

PERHAPS THE MOST RELEVANT and most deeply felt dissatisfaction in our culture is the ungroundedness of our sexual lives. In the attempt to elevate our minds, we have split love from sexuality. To make things worse, we have categorized sexual assertion and sexual receptivity, inappropriately tying them to male and female roles.

In one way or another, many of us have arrested our development in the areas of both sexuality and love, and we are unable to understand and express what gives us satisfaction. We are bewildered by questions of orgasm, perversion, and the meaning of our sexual existence. We are confused about what constitutes creative self-expression and what is damaging to self and others. It is our lack of self-contact that permits the acting-out of images which hurt us.

I see human sexuality as an ongoing process that dynamically deepens throughout an entire lifetime —when encouraged to. The evidence seems to be that our growth is linked to our having more sexual energy than we can feasibly express by having children. This surplus energy can be expended in licentiousness, scattered in superficial sexual games, or can go toward the deepening of our pleasure as we create ourselves and develop relationships.

To contain our energy is to embrace our excitement bodily, to let feelings unfold within our containing body and to let our selves be formed by these feelings. By living with and from our bodily feelings, they change us, culturing our love.

The biological development of the individual is downward, toward the ground. The child's oral needs are taken care of, the arms become free and begin to explore the world; the legs kick and gain strength for independence. There is a polarization that takes place anatomically with the enriching blood supply in the lower part of the body. We begin to feel and to be able to control areas of the body that were previously beyond us, such as the bladder, the anal sphincter, the legs and toes.

In the child, the first commitment of the heart is to the head, the mouth. But gradually its commitment descends to the genitals and legs. Our sexual functioning continues to develop throughout our lives, is tied to the opening of the heart to the earth, to others of this world.

We have fostered mental images of sexuality while denying the instinctual pole of our existence, and so have become intimidated by our own urges. Our heart gets overruled by the brain, its energy going to the life of the mind.

In a very real way we segment our bodies, twisting them according to mistaken ideas of what we are or should be. We teach ourselves not to move, not to express our thoughts and feelings. People come to me who have feelings, who think their own thoughts, but are unable to give them expression. They wage a war between inside and outside and settle for an incomplete existence. Others are unwilling to express their good feelings. They will not melt or trust.

One woman that I worked with reported that she cried silently and seldom. After all, who would answer her? She protected herself by being hard. She said that when she began to have feeling, she was at the mercy of an unknown self. She was scared to soften. Instead, she would stiffen her legs, pelvis, and diaphragm—which had the effect of severely restricting her orgastic expression. She had been taught and had taught herself from early childhood how not to cry, how not to trust her body, and she'd given up hope of reaching out to communicate.

As we grow older we learn further distortions of the life process. We live in a world of hyped-up sexual stimulation where women are taught to tease and seduce and submit, to be in what I call a clitoral state; a world where men are taught to please (to please equals potency) and to base their feelings on an "end-of-penis" experience. We orient ourselves sexually toward a splashing, sparkling, and tingling that may electrify us but does not involve our truths. Our stimulations come from the surface, in contrast to the pulsations of our organs which come from the inside.

In a workshop I conducted, there was a girl who came to experiencing the pleasure within her. This made her anxious. It was perfectly all right for her to have sensations on her skin and on her surface, but it was not all right to have feelings and pulsations on her insides. Inner sensations and movements made her very uneasy. She had learned to be ashamed of her own inwardness. This shame prevented her innards from giving sexual pleasure, and she was left with a feeling of being gypped in life, with an underlying attitude of desperation.

We have created images and other advertisements of what to expect from sexuality, and these, combined with our frustrations and longings, cause us to resort to hard, willful sexual movements. These violent movements are an attempt to unlock our contracted bodies. But they don't work. We can't achieve what is satisfying by willfully banging and pushing. The result is even less feeling, more ungroundedness.

Our desires are the basis for entering or being entered. The movement is gentle in the beginning, the two pelvises discovering and responding to each other; then it becomes more intense and insistent. Feeling finds its way to expression. There is no hysterical thrashing but rather a simple pulsating. Pulsations develop until there is an acme, a climax, and we are submerged in our ground. Self-expression is the key.

In both the woman and the man, movement originates spontaneously and develops on its own. Our bodies direct themselves, needing no direction from social images. We become involved in and move with the flow of excitement and feeling. The orgastic experience can best be appreciated by what happens after the event. Natural expression leaves a person feeling joyful, sad, awed, or aware of the other in a new way. This is in strong contrast to anger after the partial involvement which the thrashing, hysterical performance tries to overcome. Satisfaction does not come from a job well done; it comes from experiencing deeply.

It is in the sexual arena that we encounter the greatest confusion concerning positions and roles, pleasures and satisfactions. The natural development of sexuality allows a variety of roles and positions to express one's pleasures. Self-expression gives the greatest satisfaction, not techniques for bigger and better orgasms. Not everybody wants Mount Vesuvius.

We can see the consequences of partial involvement, be they of the lower body or of the upper body—or be they those brought about by acting out some learned role or living out some fantasy. Men, for example, are taught to be heroes, performers, to hold back emotion, to change things rather than to be changed by them. Generally they come to resent this. They experience the conflict of wanting to be loved on the one hand but being unwilling, physically and emotionally, to be receptive. Many women are taught to be aggressive in the world and passive in bed, another conflict that is difficult to endure. An aggressive woman who tries to act out a passive role in bed may in fact end up being hostile because she has had to disguise her assertiveness. The man experiences powerlessness because he can't get her to participate. Men humiliate women by carrying aggressive attitudes into bed, overruling the tenderness that may be called for. Oftentimes they won't allow themselves to be tender for fear of arousing the woman's assertiveness. Yet this fear is groundless; assertiveness is not an act of will, but the natural inclination of the tissue to go forward, seeking satisfaction. If natural forwardness is inhibited in man or woman, we see it expressed as a passive pelvis, or as a pelvis that has to be willfully driven to express the heart that cannot reach out.

We move through life doing whatever work we are doing—walking, washing dishes—bathed in the feelings which spread out from us to generate our atmosphere. And we share this soup with the persons we choose to be with. It is from our interaction with our own atmosphere of feelings that our excitement increases, as increased sexuality.

We invite people into our atmosphere, and we are invited into the atmospheres of others. This commingling of atmospheres and bodies deepens our commitment to each other and nourishes our ground. One always knows it when one walks into a house where people love. One literally walks into their loving atmosphere.

What I'm describing is the process in which we communicate with the earth and with others, the process that gives us a sense of us as bodies.

A life-style capable of being rooted in our biological truth, has not been encouraged. We are not taught that our bodies are our ground. Rather we are taught to live in fear of our bodies. We are taught to control and manipulate our bodies, to bully them. We are taught that our bodies are animals that require discipline. And so we never learn that our world develops from our bodily life.

Coming Home

OUR MOVEMENT DOWNWARD keeps open the top of the body to receive the gift of God. When we start to ground ourselves, basics begin to be found. When our inner movements begin to intensify, we experience a change in both our perceptions and our values.

One time a young man came to me for help. He was stuffed up, crowded into his shoulders and throat and neck like an over-padded football player. He told me he wanted to discover what he would really like to do. But he was so tight in his shoulders and neck and arms that it was almost impossible to make a dent in his protective structure. We started by working with his legs. I began systematically to use my hands to help bring excitation into his legs and feet, and then I asked him to stand on his feet so that the excitement could stream down. Slowly, as he began to experience his ground, his shoulders and arms began to descend. He stopped holding himself up. His throat opened and his voice came forth, uttering sounds that he had never made before.

He let go of the cramp in his brain that he said came from trying to figure out what to be to please his mother and father. In so doing, he found that he had sexual feelings toward his mother and that, in turn, his mother was seductive toward him. So although he wanted to please her, he didn't dare please her too much; nor did he dare to leave her. Later on in our work, when he was better able to bear his own excitation, he also understood that his father, who was constantly critical, had never permitted him to form a ground of his own. But this situation was changing. The more his excitement streamed through his body into his legs and feet, the more he established a rapport with the ground—his ground. And the more he began to form poetic images and spontaneous feelings which he was then able to infuse into his work and his relationships.

When we are grounded, we allow life to happen. We develop a quality of aliveness that changes us and our relationship with the world. Our aliveness becomes our central value. The central purpose of our living becomes that of transmitting our aliveness, our humanity, our love.

At present we teach our children to hold back and contract rather than to contain and contact. We teach by discipline, punishment, spasm—or by over-permissiveness—rather than by methods which encourage a bodily self. We don't teach our children to ground themselves in themselves. We teach them to ground themselves in others.

As I become more connected to my grounding, I work for myself not against myself. As I become more conscious of my grounding, I release myself from my childhood inhibitions without destroying my child. As I continue to ground myself, I become wider and deepen myself and my world, enhancing my love of self and others. This deepening and culturing of our caring is our humanness. Learning to find ways to express these feelings, to ground them, gives the fruit of self-realization and satisfaction.

WORKING
WITH OTHERS

Sexual

Responsiveness

I'LL TELL YOU a little bit about how I work. I use active techniques meant to mobilize you, energetically and instinctually. I use these methods because they are effective ways to get you to experience kicking, hitting, protesting, screaming, reaching, sighing, breathing, pleasuring—and to feel the accompanying emotions that can make this behavior meaningful for you.

D.H. Lawrence said, "The child kicks his way to freedom." The child kicks his way out of the dependency situation by using his legs, the organs of independence. Self-assertion is the approach I use. Kick your way to being.

The kind of movement I'm interested in is involuntary. It's not something that you can learn by practice, like gymnastics or ballet. It's something that grows out of your instinctive and emotional excitement.

My model is an orgastic model because orgasm is, for me, the event which gives us the capacity for making deepest contact. It's also a model for continuous living, a guide to being able to contain and express feeling.

An orgastic process includes the build-up and expression of energy, a pulsatory way of being in the world, of being alive. It allows feelings to move through and regulate your life, feelings that you can share with other people—or even discharge alone —deepening contact with your world.

How this happens—the multitude of patterns, of ways of being in the world—is unique and beautiful to observe. Each person has his own way of building and expressing energy and moving and contacting in the world that leads him to a satisfying sexuality. In this way, each of us incubates himself.

The efficacy of this approach is a reflection of the times. The dominant mood today is one of protest. We are actively challenging the assumptions of an industrial and puritanical age. We are in such a position today that we have to protest to begin to find our freedom. Let's begin protesting by talking.

Let's talk about the relationships between men and women. Man's biological drive is tied to woman. His independence consists in breaking this tie, so that he is no longer servicing her. I think that with most men there is a fundamental resentment of sexuality, resentment that they are dependent on the woman. So there has been a lot of experimentation with religious denial. The formula is: to deny the woman is to gain your freedom. Later on it changes: to control the woman is to maintain your freedom. This leads to the concept that further freedom is gained by controlling nature. And you can see that that's exactly what man has done—he has dominated the earth, abused it, smashed it and reshaped it. In the process he has cut himself off from his very foundations.

These concepts about the inferior place of the woman have made it easy for the man to abuse her. In compensation for his abuse, he idealizes her—not as a person, but as an imagined creature. Meanwhile he keeps on trying to control her sexuality and the sexuality of life.

On her side, the woman feels her drive is tied to man's. She feels that she has to service him, submit to him, refrain from being aggressive. "Only men should assert themselves." To protest this role, a woman has to accept her own assertiveness.

Woman: When a woman makes a forthright demand to be serviced by a man, what is he saying about himself if he responds with a feeling of resentment because he feels it's threatening to his independence?

Stan: Hey, that's a loaded question. Why should anybody service anybody? Constant servicing makes for guilt and resentment in all relationships. Any man who is servicing a woman is a dependent man. No man need service a woman, nor vice versa. What we see today, as a statement of individual strength, is: "Let's play gas station attendant; I service you, you service me." But this is not an expression of individuality. Servicing does not encourage growth.

From my point of view, when a woman makes a demand on a man, he can either respond or not respond. He shouldn't feel he has to perform for her or satisfy her.

We all have some guilt in us, no matter how healthy we are. But dealing with guilt and resentment in a positive way is really an adventure, because every time we deal with them legitimately we broaden and deepen our horizons.

If two people are able to follow their own sexual feelings, theirs is a maturing, developing relationship, not a repetitive satisfaction. There is a whole way of being alive that expresses appetite and this is what a woman may experience as desire. A man can respond to that kind of desire, and when he does they will both be able to take care of themselves. In the act of moving the woman will be able to support her own feelings and carry herself and express herself, and so will the man.

Woman: My sexual satisfaction is my responsibility and his sexual satisfaction is his responsibility?

Stan: Right. If I expect you to satisfy me, then I'm really saying that you're the one who's going to liberate me, that you're the one who's going to give me sexual feelings or sexual release. If I'm waiting to see my girl because I expect that she will turn me on, where is *my* feeling?

Woman: It sounds as if each person should just be out for what he can get. You don't mean that, do you?

Stan: On one level, that's exactly what I mean. To self-service is to be self-expressive, to be contactful and communicative. To be able to satisfy yourself, to be self-expressive, helps you understand another's rhythms. In this way, we grasp the roots of cooperation.

Woman: When you're thinking of yourself first, doesn't that imply that you are getting pleasure by thinking of the needs of your partner as well?

Stan: On the deepest level, sexuality is impersonal.

Woman: The orgasm is.

Stan: I said nothing about orgasm, I said sexuality. On the deepest level, the charging and discharging of the organism is an impersonal process. Life wants to reproduce itself. It is absolutely selfish. This is the one fact that people cannot accept, yet it is true. We can proceed from here but this has to be accepted first. There's no use in painting ideal pictures. The fact of sexual impersonality is so central, so rock-bottom, that if it is not accepted, everything else is screwed up.

Woman: Well, if we're so driven, how come we can block it off so easily?

Stan: So easily? I don't think that it's so easy to block it off. I've worked with too many people who were experiencing misery from trying to deflect the reproductive drive. That misery that's locked up inside—you think that's easy to bear? So many of us are running around in the world looking for some kind of gratification and not knowing what the hell we want.

My point is that if you can really accept and enjoy the impersonality that is in you, then you can grasp your humanity. Sexuality is impersonal. *You* make it personal.

Sexuality moves toward reproducing and expressing itself and satisfying itself with lust. This has to be experienced. And on the basis of this insistent drive, you construct your person. Your independence relies on the life process which also maintains your personality—and that's quite a paradox, but true. No matter how independent you are, life is sustained on life; you as person are dependent on this elan, and it is the source of your independence. All the riches and all of whatever else you have don't really give you independence.

Man: Can a man be deeply involved with a woman and at the same time be excited by many women?

Stan: Sure.

Man: And it might be abnormal *not* to be.

Stan: That's right, and a woman may be turned on by many men. An extension of that question is: where is the greatest *depth* of satisfaction?

Man: Is it true that the more animal-like the expression of sexuality, the more healthy and satisfying it is? In other words, do we want to get away from superimposing the mind on this animal-like act, so that we can conduct ourselves in a genuine animal fashion in our sexual relationships?

Stan: Why restrict it to sexuality? Let's say you want to relate to the world like an animal. Now, what kind of picture do you have in your head about animals?

Man: An unthinking creature.

Stan: That's what I thought. I'll tell you a story about "unthinking" animals. I saw one of the most fantastic things of my life in the Sea of Cortez off Baja California. The ship captain said to me, "You'll see the porpoises come over to the ship and play in the wake of the ship." I said that was pretty hard for me to accept; how did they understand that the ship makes waves? But sure enough, it happened half a dozen times, and the way they did it was amazing.

The ship created a big wake at the front and the porpoises came at right angles to the ship; then they all swam up to the prow, lined up in formation and surfed on this wake. From time to time number one moved out of the way and number two jumped in. They all gave each other a chance at the front. Who the hell taught them that? And this is the most startling part of all. As the wake moved out, it got weaker. On the fringes were mother fish with babies, teaching them to ride the wake.

That's unthinking? That's not being aware? or concerned? or interactive? The porpoises taught me this: *Intelligence is instinctive aliveness.*

When you really let go of yourself and make love instinctively, you'll be surprised and delighted by what it is to be a human animal. Some of the greatest poems have been written about the act of sexual loving.

Hunger and Fulfillment

MOST OF US choose a mate, a partner, out of a sense of aloneness and frustration. We're hung up in such a basic way that it partly blinds our choice. Most of us are so ashamed and shy that we just want someone to accept us.

Once we are no longer ashamed of our instinctual hungers and our bodily needs, the connections we make with others have a very different kind of eventfulness. We choose to be with those whose rhythm is related to ours in some respect; our sexual choice is that of mutual satisfaction and growth, not that of catering to each other's hungers.

One time I worked with a couple. The man's niceness was carrying a high charge of hostility, a high charge of inner rebellion. He was nice because he wanted to be serviced. He felt that his sexual assertiveness was not right. From the woman's side, she serviced him out of the fear of being abandoned. She wanted that servicing business: I do you, you do me. That kind of business doesn't work. Sexuality is not servicing. And it didn't work for either one of them. Their sexual choices were not made on the basis of mutual desire.

Sexuality that is satisfying, to any degree, is not solely dependent on the other person. It's an event of two worlds coming together, each with its own feelings, its own needs.

Many people come together who have very strong inhibitions, each agreeing to accept the other's limitations and their negative consequences. For example: "I have premature ejaculation, so you'll have to put up with that." "Okay, I accept your premature ejaculation because I can't come," or "because I'm afraid of how I feel with a man." We get this kind of arrangement instead of: "I have my pleasure, you have yours, and we come together and build on that."

Compromises may seem like good solutions for your hunger, but if you have a lot of desire your compromise won't work. Desire is living. Longing, reaching out, wanting are native to being alive and if we do anything to stop those feelings—even when there doesn't seem to be a chance for fulfillment—we cut off our willingness to live. Maturity is being willing to live with our hungers and yearnings.

A lot of times the desire in children is so deep that they simply cannot bear it, because there is nobody around to respond contactfully. Then they have no choice but to block it off, to freeze up. But to be alive is to be in contact with one's desires. This is how we connect with things. Otherwise, life is a wild search with more and more fantasy activity to compensate for our lack of fulfillment.

(To a woman who had worked earlier): I saw you allow your excitement and desire to exist in your mouth and arms. Can you allow that yearning to be in your pelvis, in the uterus? Restricting excitement to your mouth and arms doesn't permit you to act like a woman. That's why you feel empty. Allowing your yearning to move downward allows you to fill yourself, instead of filling yourself from other people.

What is it that stops me from eating a loaf of bread now, no matter how hungry I am, if I know that in an hour a luscious steak is coming out of the broiler? The containment of my hunger motivates me in a very positive way.

Woman: I can't relate this to personal relationships.

Stan: Okay. Here's an example. I am in a seminar, in which I am getting excited. There's a lot of movement in me, a buildup of sexuality. I feel that I'm an assertive man, I can have what I want and I know how to get it.

And yet I know from experience that, unless I care for somebody, I'm going to be basically unhappy if I just use her to relieve myself for the moment. The willingness to contain my feeling (and not see it as something that's torturing me and must be gotten rid of) creates an anticipatory sense, a hunger that moves

toward the best possible fulfillment. Not any fulfillment, but the most satisfying. The postponing is itself
pleasurable when it means that my feeling is deepening. But looking for an *ideal* person to make contact
with is also crazy. You do that and you'll lie on your
death-bed one day with a hungry tongue.

You have to farm it. I'd rather use an agricultural
model instead of a technological model because technology doesn't lead me anywhere. It creates greater
convenience, but no livingness.

We can take what we have and begin to farm it
and deepen it and live the joys and frustrations of the
farmer. In a workshop like this we are planting seeds,
possibilities, but you have to take to farming yourself.
The seed is in all of us. It's there.

We're talking here about the ground of life, which
is sexuality. Sexuality is not the center of life. The
center we call love. The head has been more than
successful in seducing the loyalty of the heart. As long
as the center is forced to serve the white god in the
mountains, and neglects the roots and the soil, we're
in trouble.

Guilt and Trust

THERE ARE PEOPLE who have made up their minds that the whole world is a pile of dung. That nothing is real. That feelings are to be manipulated and to be taken advantage of. That feelings don't really count. I don't say that they do that manipulating consciously, but they surely do it.

If these people could feel how tender the body can be, how decent it is, then the rest of their defensive rigidity might be unnecessary.

Get to your feeling, and it will begin to act as a resonator. You will begin to *experience* what is real, what is worthwhile. And from that place you can begin to grow. But if the bodily experience is not there, then everything becomes subject to challenge and denial, and there is nowhere to go. The way that we are in the world depends fundamentally on the quality of aliveness in our tissue.

Man: That woman you just worked with was in such complete control most of the time that she could hardly cry. Her crying was just a few sniffles and that's all.

Stan: Did you hear the crying and anger both coming out at the same time? It sounded like the anger of a child left alone.

She says she was raised in a convent, but she is spoiled, overindulged. They played a game with her: "We love you, and God loves you. We'll give you the goodies if you'll give up your life."

Man: I thought that she gave up her bodiliness every time she started to intellectualize.

Stan: She was most real when she said "No—no, I don't want it from them." Generally she gets things from others. She is a person who has been able to sexualize all aspects of her life, and she uses this sexuality to manipulate people.

Woman: What's so unusual about that?

Stan: Well, how many people do you know who let themselves consciously feel how they use their sexuality to get favors from others? At least she has the guts to say where it's at for her. But she has guilt with it. Her guilt comes from misusing herself. Guilt is such a basic statement of "I am not me" that to attribute it to moral or educational history alone is to miss the issue entirely. To explain the guilt as deriving from her years in a convent or from moralistic attitudes toward sex wouldn't change anything. What is important is her unwillingness, her inability to experience her body and accept it.

There are two kinds of guilt. One is the guilt that I lay on you: the "don't be" variety—don't be sexual, don't be dumb; all that moralism which you submit to. The guilt is that of angry submission.

There's another kind of guilt, and that's existential guilt: the guilt of not being who you are, that of betraying yourself. This is a guilt that we all live with. How do they postulate original sin and get everybody to accept it? It's because it's built on an inner perception, it has a ring of truth for people. We *experience* our inner guilt because we sense our unfinishedness, our incompleteness.

But once you grasp the idea that all of us are incomplete, that we're not closed biological systems, that we're open-ended, then you realize that there must always be a feeling of incompleteness.

It's from this feeling that we may get the sense that something is wrong. But nothing is wrong; we simply want to be more ourselves. The less we program ourselves, the less we experience this guilty feeling.

This feeling of being incomplete is a basic feeling and one of the motive forces in our lives. It is an accurate feeling. We're incomplete, moving toward more and more completion and connection. To the degree that we betray that ongoingness, we feel guilt.

"And man is a promise, he is not yet." That's a line from the Old Testament that antedates the humanistic movement by thousands of years. You are a promise. You are not yet. And what we do to move ourselves away from our promise produces guilt.

Man: When you were talking about religion, you said that it was based on something quite natural, namely, that the sense of incompletion could create guilt and that the belief in original sin was in turn based on this guilt. Yet there are cultures that see this incompletion as a beautiful cosmic oneness with the universe.

Stan: I completely agree. We have used the experience of incompletion in a particular way. Our philosophy has produced the most marvelous technology in the world. The accomplishments we have made are stupendous; there's no denying that. So there is a certain validity in how we've approached our problems. I don't want to wipe that out. We have done something of which we can rightly be proud.

We have accomplished something, yet at the same time we accuse ourselves of being failures. But if we are a failure, we are a beautiful one. And I take strength in that. We don't have to feel guilty for our incompleteness.

Many people have the idea that beauty is archetypal, a goal to be met. But we don't need an unchanging ideal to live up to. Life expresses itself for what it is, and that in itself is quite beautiful. We don't have to be successful; we can be failures, and we can be magnificent failures.

In the last of his books, the historian Spengler says something that will make this clearer. He points out the relationship between advanced technology and the dying of a culture. Each culture that has developed a sophisticated technology has died and disappeared soon after. He makes the point that our society is calling for more and more specialists in engineering and mechanics and so forth—which is an indication to him of our dying. So his advice to young men is to live their destiny and become engineers.

Woman: But that would put you out of business.

Stan: That's okay, because life is bigger than me, and bigger than anything I do. That's exactly what I'm talking about. If we're in a dying culture, live the death. In all the work I've done on myself, there comes a point at which I realize there are things that are never meant to be overcome, but lived with, experienced. If a tree is growing straight up and something happens that causes it to bend, that bend becomes part of its existence. Life is what it is. It becomes by expressing itself. If I live my existence, there's a beauty in that living.

We cannot remove the mystery. Look at the history of our science: the more we plunge, the more mystery we find. Every veil lifted reveals other veils in an unending chain of deepening. I'm not implying that we should not try to lift the next veil, but I'm saying that how we go about it is very important. Many people mistake dissection for penetration, but pulling something apart doesn't necessarily mean that you have penetrated and understood.

The fact that a man enters a woman's vagina doesn't mean that he understands anything. He might be so hung up on getting in there that he can't experience anything except polishing the struggle of penetrating.

Man: What you're really saying is that to solve the mystery we have to learn to depend on life.

Stan: You don't solve mysteries. You live with them. You learn to depend upon mysteries, and to trust them.

Let's make it more practical. Let's take it right down to sexuality and what happens there.

What makes an erection? One trusts, and when we don't have that trust, we have to use all kinds of gimmicks. The act of penetration is accomplished by the man with a stiff penis. Once the penis has entered, the aggressive, penetrating quality comes to be more in balance with the quality of tenderness. The penis becomes a little less hard. Most men who experience this partial softening fear losing their potency, and sometimes they actually do. They lose their trust in their feeling. The standards for potency that the ego operates by are different from the actual feelings.

We are so accustomed to a performing attitude toward life that we even superimpose it on our sexual function. We have lost trust in our bodies. To be in touch with our bodies is to trust, and every contraction is saying: I don't trust. To contract is to distance ourselves from our ground.

Without knowing it, people live their lives on that lack of trust: I don't know whether I can trust me as body, I don't know whether I can accept myself. To make that decision and live that life is a physiological experience. Every step is based on a lack of trust in what will emerge. But the minute that you begin to open your body and allow your feelings to emerge, you can then begin to make that part of your life by acting on it. Acting on it creates form, life structure. Then you die again and allow something else to emerge and structure that. Our lives continue forming in this way.

Self-discovery experiences in my life have occurred when I have allowed myself to be with what is. It is then that I have my shyness and my poet—a new part of me—and hey, that's a surprise, and this is a surprise. Experiences bubble up like a rich fountain that never runs dry. This bubbling up is more than the tension of need. It reveals the excitement of the whole dynamic of living.

Being with what is is trust of the deepest kind. And as trust builds up, there is a stage at which we begin to softly emerge, if we're not too scared. We emerge from a cloud of unknowing into more and more clarity; and as we emerge, we gain more and more identity of who we are. This is how we build inner trust. The same holds true for relationships. We all come from a place of seemingly little self-identity, but there is a paradox in that our form is our identity, and it is innately aware of itself. So we are never without our identity; we never lose it. As we emerge we simply realize it more and more.

I see life as a spiral that unfolds. The more we are in touch with ourselves, the more mystery there is to life. I can't really describe what it means; it's what is revealed over a lifetime. The bodily life is a deepening process, the essence of a person's life experience. Is it transmitted in some way in the germ plasma? Is it possible that the personality's interaction with the instinctual life, and vice-versa, affects one's genetic code? Is this the process of evolution? Is one of the functions of maturing to transmit our experiences to our offspring? If so, what does this mean in relation to our system of education? Does sending kids to school really educate them? What do they acquire when they are force-fed? Being force-fed leads to guilt and a lack of trust in one's impulses. Learning means to acquire something one desires, to make it one's own.

How would an educator who doesn't provoke guilt or distrust in regard to bodily processes go about educating a child? What kind of science would be created by a scientist who is deeply embedded in his instinctual feelings? Living life instinctually and dynamically builds trust and diminishes guilt, giving us quite a different perspective.

Nudity and Privacy

HERE IN AMERICA there seems to be an escalating diminution of our privacy. Lately there has arisen the phenomenon of encouraging people to make public confessions in groups, and to be up front with all aspects of their lives. The group phenomenon has come about partly for financial reasons: people resent paying forty dollars an hour. Also there aren't enough therapists to go around, and there's an argument that the one-to-one relationship is artificial, that therapy needs to return to a family setting. In the next four chapters we'll consider these questions, and perhaps create a more organic perspective about them.

The issue of what privacy means relative to personal power has never been discussed. Strip a man of his privacy, and you strip him of his power. Make everything public and explicit, remove the mystery, and you threaten the sources of individuation. Group nudity is an attempt to take away one's privacy, and as such it's a threat to one's power.

Our ideas about what constitutes growth-enhancing group behavior may change radically when people become more intact, more in touch with themselves. The present therapeutic group need not be the model for group contact, group dynamics. Once when I had a lot of difficulty in relating to a group, I understood that I was trying to relate out of one state, and they were trying to relate out of another state. We were in two different places. I knew that I could be open and revealing, but how involved did I have to get with everyone I came into contact with? I wanted to be part of the group without necessarily having to violate my sense of privacy.

Woman: Do you believe that parents should have sexual intercourse in front of their children and be nude in front of them?

Stan: Both of these things certainly happen, but I don't advocate sex in front of children. In our culture it is damaging.

Woman: Even the nudity?

Stan: To a point. I heard R.D. Laing once say that the reason the sex scene between parents is traumatic for children is that they do not see love making; but an act of violence. I think a lot of family nudity can be traumatic to children for the same reason. People parade their nudity and impose it on everybody else, trying to force others to give them the acceptance they cannot give themselves.

There may be nudity in the family, but it's often too big a burden for the kid to carry into the school-world situation. It can create conflict in the child which he may not be able to deal with.

For a child to take any kind of sexual intimacy into the established world can become a burden to him. The taboo is overwhelming. Parents have to prepare their children for the discrepancy between what happens at home and what happens in the outside world. But even so, where do you draw the line? How do you stop a child from being sexually intimate with his sister, or with his parents? In either situation secretiveness develops, and secretiveness gets mistaken for privacy. Secretiveness is non-communicative. Privacy involves discreet communication.

The trouble with nudity is that many times, by going naked in front of a child, the parent is really trying to seduce that child. It happens enough with the clothes on. The parent excites the poor kid completely out of proportion to what the kid can bear.

Man: What do you think of nudity in groups?

Stan: Extremes in any direction create problems. Dictatorships forbid public nudity in an effort to force people into a clothed impersonality. The licentious carnivals of old invited people into a naked impersonality. Any socially imposed extreme rapes individual privacy.

My own personal experience of group nudity, in the hot baths at the Esalen Institute growth center, always left me feeling less than comfortable. I did begin to discover deeper and more interesting levels of shyness in myself, and some places of shame. On the other hand, I didn't like the voyeuristic attitude. Some people can put up with that, but I didn't like being ogled. That's number one. I didn't want to abandon my reserve in order to be part of the group; that's number two. And three, I felt that the situation robbed me of my privacy.

Group nudity can lead to group touching and group sexuality. Where does one become arbitrary in all this? I want to have something to say about who touches me and whom I touch. Besides, I find that a private intimacy heightens my feelings. To globalize my feelings robs them of their focus.

Now, there are some people who simply enjoy being naked with others. But there are also people who need this kind of scene. There are people who need this kind of exposure to overcome deep feelings of shame or inhibition. In an attempt to overcome their inhibitions, they allow themselves to become desensitized, which robs their life of its mystery. And then there are other people who just love to flood their whole experience with obscenity and pornography.

Man: I was at a party once where all the people took off their clothes and went swimming in the nude. I couldn't feel comfortable because they were acting out a lot of their emotional needs and problems. If they could have taken off their clothes casually, I could easily have been one of them. If there was no exaggerated significance to it, fine. But I felt that because I didn't want to take off my clothes, and they were waiting to observe me, it was an infantile kind of thing, and I was reluctant to expose myself. I refused on the grounds that this was morbid.

Stan: Sexual expression that two or three people want between themselves is one thing, but to force this on others is quite another thing. The minute you want to make it public, you begin to pressure and condemn those who don't wish to engage. If you want to take a distorted state and establish that as the norm, I will not buy it. Don't be seduced into accepting infantility as a norm. That's crazy.

Man: I don't want to expose my child or myself to the voyeur, but I want to be able to expose my healthy body. I want to say to my child that this me, this whole me, is healthy. And at the same time I want to minimize the effect of the pressure he is going to be under when he steps outside the apartment.

Stan: Well, I know that if a woman and a man have a good sexual relationship they don't have to worry too much about laying things on the child. And if a woman is without a man, but is aware of herself, she will not lay things on her son. She will maintain a distance from the child, and while that's a tragedy, it's nevertheless a necessity. The same thing goes for fathers and daughters.

Man: Isn't it somewhat unhealthy not to be able to bare your body without feeling shame and revulsion in doing it?

Stan: No, that shame and revulsion is not necessarily unhealthy. A lot of times in groups, or in families, there is such a pervasive feeling of self-dislike and worthlessness in regard to bodies that it's very unpleasant to be around. Have you ever been in a whorehouse? It's depressing. Have you ever touched an unloved body in an intimate way? The human being who is alive is sensitive to other people. An alive body is vulnerable to the feeling of others.

Man: Are you equating exposure in a whorehouse with exposure of your body in a group?

Stan: There are alot of similarities. Look for example at dancing. It's implied that there are sexual feelings built up in that dancing. But it's a sham. The dancers are not sexual. They are imitating sexual fantasies, using their bodies as instruments; they're not building sexual feelings. And I dislike this distortion.

When one's body is alive one develops strong likes and dislikes. One is sensitive to perversions of living. Strength is the ability to react and deal with situations in the most life-positive way. An instinctually responsive person will either protest a negative situation, or walk away, or die a little.

When I'm working with somebody whose body is disturbed, I have my own responses. I may be able to accept the unhealthiness in that person, but that doesn't mean I like it. My dislike mobilizes my desire to try to understand and interfere. This is part of the healing process. What I don't like keeps me at a distance; if I want to decrease the distance I have to try to understand or alter what I don't like.

Man: Are you saying that I have to restrain my sexuality?

Stan: You're missing the point. Many primitive

people cover their genitals. Why? There is no need for them to do it. Have you seen the shyness that is there quite naturally in children, especially as they begin to develop a sense of privacy about their bodies—like not wanting to be touched or kissed?

Most religions have had the carnival, where they have permitted impersonal sexuality to occur—the unbridled satisfying of all lusts. But anonymity was a requisite. What would happen if we always had a circus? We would lose the development of personal intimacy. Losing one's privacy results in impersonalness.

When an adult person continually behaves like a child with another person, something is cuckoo. When an adult's sexual satisfaction comes mostly from looking, or from sucking, then something is not right.

Now, I wish to live my adult sexuality. I don't wish to continually engage in adolescent sexuality, where "x" amount of nudism and "x" amount of exhibitionism may be necessary for arousal. If some people need that, fine. But I can't see myself going to bed with a woman who is the equivalent of a fifteen-year-old girl, whom I could never satisfy myself with. I choose not to use myself that way.

I see a positive side to reticence and shyness—it's not all negative. A lot of my feelings are private. I contain them, and then I choose to share them with one or two or three people. I don't choose to make a public display of myself.

Woman: As I sit here I just get angrier and angrier. I don't think I ever tried to arouse my son sexually. I was persuaded against my feelings to be nude in my home. I never felt comfortable.

Stan: Then why did you listen to somebody else's idea? Direct your anger at that person and see that your anger is also a statement of your own betrayal of yourself.

Fathers, Mothers, Daughters, Sons

THE MOVEMENT OF CHILDHOOD is from dependency to being more independent, more individualistic. If the father and the mother are not accepting of the child's normal challenge of parental values, then the only way open to the child is a combination of submission and defiance: being willful and at the same time being secretive about it. The child uses the energy of his developing to support that defiance, and then equates masculine or feminine strength with its intensity, rather than with the extent of sexual feelings. Instead of letting the sexual feelings find their own expression, the child robs these feelings to feed the defiant attitude.

This man to my left, who's just been working in the group, reveals defiance in the stiffness of his spine and neck. It's as if he has a steel rod through him. His jaw is pulled back and his teeth are clenched. His face is grim. His buttocks and abdomen are pinched tight. His breath is short and shallow. His emotional expression is "I won't, you can't make me"—which serves to defend against his needs for contact and his feelings of love. The rigidities keep him from the *yes* of his natural movement, which would be to reach out.

To maintain his attitude of defiance, he diverts the downwardness of this sexual energy. This energy frightens him, so he stiffens up rather than allowing it to fill him. And in this way his masculinity converts into his defiant stance.

How the parents relate to a child's move from dependency to increasing independence is crucial. The father both prepares the male child and becomes the object of his challenge. Through challenging his father, the boy mobilizes his masculine energy for the environmental tasks he'll be facing. And if the father rejects this assertiveness, he undermines the kid's confidence. You can't teach a child to be a man; you have to be one yourself. If a man is not afraid of his own assertiveness, he won't discourage the challenges of his son.

The same thing goes for a woman and her daughter. If a woman is secure in her own assertive femininity, she doesn't discourage this quality in her daughter.

Man who has been working: The thing that moved me was when you asked me to make a loud sound as I exhaled. That really broke up the shells and fences around me.

Stan: My hunch is that, for you, success at this time would be your worst enemy. Then you'd feel you can do it, and that feeling of overconfidence has all too often been your undoing.

One way for you to deepen your feelings is to experience the nature of your tragedy. Nobody can help you until you accept that your stiffness chokes your own emotional life.

We got somewhere when I didn't participate in the contest you were setting up. I went around your competitive attitude, just kept moving away from it, and all of a sudden we weren't in a contest any more. You felt lost, and that helped.

To say to your father, "Love me," is what you wanted. But instead, with your stiffness and your drive to succeed, you've tried to win your father's love and, at the same time, to defeat your own need for it. What has dawned on you is that success is your defense. So the essence of working with you from now on is to encourage the opposite—not failure, but learning not to compete; learning to let things happen rather than to make things happen. That's what I tried to show you with the breathing: to let the sound come out rather than making the sound.

I wonder how many of us could come to our fathers and make that statement, that simple statement, "Daddy, this is the kind of love I need." So many of us have stood with our hearts in our mouths and looked with longing eyes at our fathers and been unwilling to say this. Instead, we say, "I'll succeed. I'll be better than you, then you'll have to love me."

But by then it's too late. Once you've earned it, who needs it.

In the child's early stages, the image of the father is painted by the mother. If the mother can accept him, then the child can. When the mother can't get along with the father, the child sees him as an enemy.

Man: My mother told me to throw my father out of the house. I was about to do it, physically, but my father was very shrewd. He said, "Don't lay a hand on me, because you'll regret it for the rest of your life." That stopped me.

Stan: He wasn't so much shrewd as direct, honest. He understood that your anger and contempt were misdirected. That's what your inflated chest says: "I'm my mother's son. She has inflated me at the expense of my father's balls."

You seem to still be suffering from the guilt of helping to castrate your father. I think it's something you haven't looked at yet. This is not to deny his responsibility; he castrated himself. But you helped.

Given a choice between father and son, why should the mother choose the son unless the father is not authentic? If she chooses the man, she does so out of the blossoming of her womanness and her individuality. If she chooses the son, it will be from her own deep feelings of fear about her womanliness, or because the husband doesn't fulfill her needs. How this choice operates in the dynamics of a family can be seen in a family I worked with. I'll describe the situation for you.

Morris was a short, heavy-set man with a large

chest and a body made strong by weightlifting from an early age. His father was an irrational man, given to bursts of outrage that made the son feel helpless and impotent. He built himself up to stand up to his father. Morris' mother was a self-sacrificing type, not athletic or physical like her husband, tending instead to be secretive and manipulative. Her husband was her problem child and her son was her favorite.

Morris became non-threatening and a controller to subdue his explosive rages when he felt he had not been appreciated for his sacrifices. He inflated himself against his father and identified with his mother's martyrdom. Morris' sister was a tall, gangling girl who early on began to deal with her father's rages by being evasive, non-confronting, blaming her brother who in turn blamed her. Yet she rejected her mother and her mother's martyred ways. She later became the bad girl, denying the demands of the family and the motherly role. Her long, concave body was strong, muscular like her father's. She took many lovers. Always the girl, she never pleased anyone. Morris tried to please his mother.

The sexual patterns of the parents were middle-European, a sado-masochistic game in which the father had to wait to be served and ended up not pleasing the woman who served him. How could he please her? He wished to be loved as a boy and treated like a man, and how could she relate to the man in someone she had to keep as a boy?

The shape of this family was concavity and ram-rod puffed-upness, like the old World's Fair ball and pyramid. Its process was attack and placation. The incestuous feelings were quite high, the boy with his mother in a secret mutual admiration game that made the father the bad guy, and the excited fear of the daughter that made for hating her father and herself. This was a family of accusers and blamers.

The father's body was flat, straight, hard, unyielding. The mother was compressed, bending and cunningly submissive. She didn't let anything in or out. The father kept trying to push in, punch in. Morris, like his mother, kept withholding. He raised his chest and pulled his pelvis back out of fear. His sister, in her broken-field run, her fragmented limb movements, never really focused on anyone. Although she longed for love, she ran from intimacy and picked men who deprecated and humiliated her. Morris picked rational, dependent women. This was a family in which nobody satisfied anybody, although all demanded to be served, taken care of and made to feel adequate. Sexuality and excitement went underground and emerged as anger and placation.

Morris had the classic puffed-up chest we see when one has had a sexually provocative mother who exaggerates her son's self-importance for her own needs. He had been inflated. An inflated person, though he looks very impressive, has an enormous investment of energy in somebody else's fantasy. He blows himself up as a protective device to keep others away, also to keep away feelings of being small and to pull away from unwanted sexual feelings. Morris had an invasive mother—and he could not say "no" to her openly. He inflated his chest and literally pulled up his balls and shrank his scrotum and this became his yes and no. If he gave in to her, he would succumb to his desire and hers. If he said no, he would be abandoned. Damned if he gave in, damned if he rejected her. So he blew up, swelled himself up to be big, to please her and to defend himself. His chest was saying, "Yes, I'm big"; his testicles said, "No, I won't be sexual." This made him mother's man, and father became the scapegoat whom he tried not to be like.

When I met the father, I got the impression of his being a little boy, and the wife being a mother to him. She was getting Morris to make her feel womanly. The father was the scapegoat and got the most energy. The most available person gets most of the attention whether it's positive or negative. Being the bad guy or the fool has its rewards. Why does the father put up with this? Because he chooses to feel like a boy.

The mother has heavy legs and buttocks and a sagging compressed chest. Her ass is passive and unmoving and I could imagine her needing sadistic sex to be aroused from her passivity. But she must be frightened of this, so she looks for other ways to overcome her depressedness. She chooses someone who will rouse her. The kids, too, have a stake in keeping her that way.

In this situation, the father's stiffness gave him a weak relationship to his ground, hence his underdeveloped maleness and his need for support. He was easily provoked and would erupt like a child. He could not contain himself. His forwardness and eruptiveness were complemented by the mother's passivity and withdrawal, her receiving of emotional energy even though she did not respond. Poor Morris had to be man to both father and mother. No wonder he was puffed up. Papa was the bad little boy, getting plenty of attention. And Morris was the hero, the idealized savior. Nobody could win. All were caught in a circle of the family rule: admire Mama, fear Papa. They all got their share of excitement, but it never led to satisfaction. All felt connected only to the extent that their infantile needs or fantasies were met.

If a woman is relating to her son as the savior, I really feel that it is the father's right to leave that house or to alter the situation dramatically. Otherwise there are three unhappy lives.

A man exercises who he is in life, and in raising children he has to find a way to do it without de-sexing them, without staging a war between his own dependency needs and their dependency needs. A woman who has a dependent man on her hands should realize that this is so; either she wants this, or she and he have to come to terms with it. If not, she will feel contempt for him, and to the degree that she feels contempt for him, she will raise her boy to share in her contempt. So if she sees that the guy isn't right for her, then she and the children are better off alone. Or else she ought to get herself a lover.

In seductive families, there is never any admission that sexual feelings are going on between parent and child, or between sister and brother; one plays dumb. To act on its reality is to bring down the wrath of the extended family and other authorities; not to act on it destroys the family connection. So tension mounts and secretiveness mounts and acting is inhibited.

In seductive families, life becomes grim. There is never really any playfulness. Everything is charged with double and triple meanings. Families that dampen excitement dampen lightness, brightness, irrationality, fun. Pleasure becomes a chore called "be happy." Children are not taught to enjoy or cooperate, they are taught to perform and compete; not to work for their own needs but to succeed, to acquire power and to dominate; to be shrewd and secretive rather than imaginative.

Ian Suttie was a Scottish analyst who talked a lot about the Oedipal situation. He said that children's incestuous feelings cannot exist in isolation, that they've got to exist in relation to the parents' sexual feelings or fantasies. It's impossible for a child to imagine having sexual intercourse or sexual connection with a parent unless that parent is also entertaining such feelings or fantasies. So the Oedipal situation is a two-way street.

The key to raising children is to have a good relationship with yourself and with the opposite sex.

If I have a satisfying relationship with my woman, then my daughter's sexual existence is affirmed by that. I am not taking my sexual dissatisfaction and directing it toward my daughter. She can present her emerging womanness, and I can say yes to it—be proud of it and not shut her off. I can say to my daughter: I love you, I accept your womanness, I accept your sexual feelings. And we can have these feelings for each other. But this doesn't mean sexual intercourse, nor does it mean sexual ties or exclusivity. I don't discourage her from having lovers. When one finds a lover, one's sexual feelings toward one's parents diminish. After all, feelings increase with expression.

Working With People

WANTING

Stan: Jean, let's try to soften the tension in your neck. We'll see if that increases the feeling connection between your head and the rest of your body.

Did you ever see a kid lying in a crib and banging his head against the mattress? Try doing that . . . You're sucking in your belly and holding yourself very tightly. That inhibits your feeling. Let yourself breathe when you do it . . . Don't be so timid. Is that all the assertiveness you can muster behind your need? Isn't it all right to want?

I see you squeezing your neck, your mouth, your abdomen, your buttocks. You're saying, "I won't reach out. I'm not going to speak up." You have stifled the voracity of your want. The only hint of it is in your

132

diffused eyes that are afraid to focus and say "I want that." Instead they beg.

Kick hard and make a demand. Say, "Give it to me!" . . . That was expressed like a little girl having a tantrum. You were forced to say "no" to your desires and needs before you were able to say "no" to your parents. They broke your will.

Would you go one more step with me? I want you to say at the top of your voice, as loud as you can, "I want!" . . . Can you hear the fear in your voice in making that statement?

What happened here, Jean, when you released the contraction in your neck which was inhibiting your wanting?

Jean: I experienced lack of push and I didn't feel together.

Stan: Her internal feeling was not enough. It needed coordination with her action system in order to be expressed.

LONGING

Stan: Millie, I feel that you're issuing a challenge to me. Let's work with that challenge and see what's going on. Can you recognize that it is in your chest? You push the chest up and hold your breath, as if to say, "Make me." You keep your tenderness away from your genitals that way . . . Open your legs a little and exhale. Let the chest soften. Let it down and let the good feelings through . . . I'm wondering if anyone has ever satisfied you?

Millie: A long time ago.

Stan: Why no more? What's missing?

Millie: A feeling of loving and being loved.

Stan: Is what you're saying, "Make me love you?" Is that the challenge? Can anybody make you love them? You talked about tenderness and satisfaction being missing . . . Breathe and let that defiance in your chest soften or you'll go on being stuck with your longing, your dream of the ideal lover who sweeps you off your feet.

Breathe into your chest and open your heart again. With your open heart, can you say goodbye to your fantasy lover—your Prince Charming who will make you love him—*you* have love feelings that you need to share.

YES AND NO

If you can't say "no" you can't say "yes." You cannot affirm something unless you have the ability to deny it. Unless you have the ability to maintain your individuality by saying "no," any "yes" that you may say is not a "yes." It's simply compliance and submission.

Giving in to somebody is not saying "yes." Giving in to your own sexuality is not saying "yes." You may just be overwhelmed.

You see, "most of our "no's" are unconscious.

They become a defense against pain, a lack of feeling. That's what happens. All your "yeses" are based on a "no" that is unspoken.

Unless you have lived with the dread of having to be alone, and on your own two feet, then you can't say "yes." The inability to say "no," this unwillingness to be alone, prevents you from saying "yes." Notice that when we're working, a remarkable thing happens. The minute you begin to say "no," the positive things begin to happen.

I could stand on my head and try to get you to say "yes" all the time—coerce you, push you, kick you—but then your "yes" doesn't mean anything. Two minutes later your affirmation collapses.

But the "no" stands. The minute you allow your ability to say "no" to emerge and you face the fear attached to saying it, many other feelings begin to develop. Look at what happened to Pat. She said "no" and her legs became wobbly—but she began to get feeling in them. On the other hand, take a guy like Hal. He never said "no" directly. He used substitutes like proving he doesn't need anybody, being determined to get ahead, undercutting people. These were all indirect expressions of his "no" that prevented him from really saying it and feeling how he had structured it.

A "no" can be a withholding by *containment*, or a withholding by contracting or grasping. Containment is a soft swelling, an expansion. Consider the chambers of the heart: they swell and expand as the blood enters. The heart doesn't hang on. Most of us learn to hold tight, to hoard, rather than to be filled. Most of us think that to say "no" is to hold back, to punish. It is not. It is to grow bigger.

SOFTENING

The spasticity and the numbing that Chris experienced as he was working looked like over-breathing to me. There was increased excitement in his body coupled with an unwillingness to act. There was a buildup of excitation which was not held back, making him rigid.

I have noticed consistently that when people freeze up they can be helped out of it by expressing themselves emotionally—kicking, or hitting, or whatever. The minute they open the door for feeling, this rigidifying reaction softens.

The stiffening comes about because there exists a fear of movement. A frightened person develops what appears to be hyperventilation, but this is only an appearance. Actually, they're experiencing withdrawal. As Jean began to act aggressively, she went rigid. This is what happens to a child when his contact is blocked. He freezes, then he may panic at his freezing and institute actions to overcome the freezing and alleviate the panic. Going rigid can be a panic response to either assertive or tender feelings. To do this, we inhibit our diaphragms. How is a person emotionally involved in something if he doesn't allow his breathing to be full?

PROTEST

What happened to Chris was very important. There was a qualitative change in the movements of his thighs and chest resulting from his assertive expressions and deep breathing. He has already begun to express his "yes" and his "no" in an entirely different way, an expression that is more instinctual. Instead of its being an immobile "no," his whole body has begun to respond.

If I were to work with him on a long-term basis, I'd have him kick until he expressed his spite actively instead of expressing the spiteful "no" of "I won't live, I won't give in to you." I would ask him to keep kicking until he mobilized what I call a "hot no," in place of that defiant, "cold no" that rejects his own life.

I would keep him kicking until he expressed his protest against being insecure. Once he does that he won't have to feel so inadequate, always turning to other men for support. He may begin to feel his own genitals, and learn to do what gives him a broadening feeling of his own manhood.

Probably his father put pressure on him to be a certain kind of man, to be productive, competitive. But he identified with his mother. Momma says: "I do everything for you, sonny boy. I want to make you happy." He learns how to be acceptable and loving to her. Then he says: "I do this for you, Mommy." He doesn't experience that his sensations are for himself.

They're for her. So, when she discourages his sexuality, he gives up his testicles like a good boy.

You heard him say, "I never said no to Mamma." He never had a confrontation with her. He just froze up.

He relates to men basically with contempt. And that must mean that he has contempt for his own manhood. He's always trying to be someone other than who he is. The minute he sees that he's in the same trap as his father, he may have a little sympathy; he may feel his own sadness and tragedy. When he's again on a feeling level, change is possible.

I tried to help him perceive how his sunken chest and his underdeveloped legs embodied his feelings of unsureness, making it difficult for him to be self-affirming. When there was movement, excitement, he began to feel stronger. I could see his legs vibrating, and I'm hoping that now he'll be able to feel his testicles.

Even in the last few minutes there was a significant change in his state of aliveness. His breathing softened and he looked more grounded. His facial grimness started to crack a little bit.

He wouldn't be too much in touch with his feelings yet. But the important thing is that he was able to get to the feeling, even though he couldn't sustain it for long.

Something I would like to call to your attention is the overall changes that people express when they work. These changes may not last long, but their effect is cumulative. Chris started out with a quality of hardness which acted as a defense against his feelings of insecurity and self-contempt. When I asked him to stand up and he got some excitement in his legs, the hard quality began to change. With Jean, the submissive quality turned into a quality of desire. I think a lot of people felt that. She experienced her body as being more unified. She went from expressing a feeling of "I don't deserve anything" to a feeling of "I'm worthwhile." And her change in feelings changed all of us.

BEGGING AND WITHHOLDING

Stan: Do you notice how you are pushing me away, warding me off with your talking?

Bev: Shall I hush?

Stan: I just want you to be aware of what you're doing.

Bev: What I feel I want to accomplish is to be able to express my own feelings and not go back to what somebody else wants and thinks is best.

Stan: Can you express your own feelings, your own demands for pleasure—in bed?

Bev: Yes, but I couldn't for a long time.

Stan: If you can do it in bed, why can't you do it in the world?

Bev: I'm beginning to.

Stan: How can you be assertive and demanding in bed and not in the rest of your life? It leads me to believe that you're not being as assertive in bed as you think you are.

I'd like you to kick assertively and see how you respond . . . I noticed a quality in you before, when you started to stand up, and now you've just affirmed it. It's a pleading quality. I see it also in your bodily limpness. Are you sure you're not mistaking that begging quality for aggressiveness? Let's work with the pleading right now. That may be the clue.

Imagine a child who hasn't learned to speak, who is being conditioned to be compliant. The child begs, silently . . . You're doing it again. You're pleading: your tone of voice, your gesture. As your voice comes to me, it jars me. You're apologizing for being alive. You do it by making yourself small, by shrinking, collapsing. Try to say, "I won't" . . . Now your shrinking is turning into anger . . . Isn't your cooperative attitude how you betray yourself?

Bev: I'm saying "Okay, I'll be cooperative, I'll listen. I'll please you," but underneath I'm saying "No!" Even to me.

Stan: Is this how you convert your good feelings into resentment and hate? Can you make a direct expression of anger, or of tenderness? Or are you going to talk and talk and spill your feelings out your mouth, self emptying, and be left with disappointment?

FANTASY OR FEELING

Do you focus on the fantasy or the feeling? Are you living in your pictures or in your feelings? Where is your focus of concentration?

All right, let's say you're going to make love. Do you call up a fantasy? Where are you—in the feeling or in the fantasy?

In a lot of things that people do, they get hung up on their fantasy. They rely on the pictures in their heads. They need the pictures to arouse themselves or they need the pictures to sustain their arousal. They stay in the pictures rather than identifying with what they are feeling. And sometimes they stay in the pictures because they have no feeling.

To substitute fantasy for feeling is to get stuck in the head. But you don't have to deny a fantasy. Let it be. Just don't focus there.

ASSERTIVENESS

Stan: No, Phil, you're not trying to give me what I want; you're trying to give me what you think I want. You're creating an illusion.

Phil: I think I know what you want, so I'll make believe I'm giving it to you, because I don't feel sure of what I've got to give.

Stan: You're trying to develop your selfhood, and your pleasing and performing is a cover for your unsureness. Why should you cover it? Unsureness is legitimate as one searches for and finds his own substance.

You've got a choice when you're working with yourself. You can fool yourself or really commit yourself. It's a matter of denying or affirming your life.

I'm not buying that deprecating smile on your face. You're pretending. Assertiveness that is available is powerful stuff. You can't deny it when it's present. It doesn't necessarily mean hostility. Assertiveness can have destructuring effects, but it's basically a positive dynamic force.

An artist destructures, he might have to say, "I have to destroy one image to create another." Or a farmer who knows he must plow the field. If I approach life like the cowardly lion, nothing is going to happen.

VIBRATION

Phil, simply say, "I need you," and let that expression move you . . . See what happens? There's spontaneous vibration. You're quivering.

That vibration is with us all the time. The more this vibration moves us, the more we're alive. The flow either intensifies or diminishes, depending on our level of commitment.

It's that flow of vibration that gives birth to feeling and expression. Anything that interferes with it, interferes with aliveness. It's a natural state. It's the same vibratory state that leads toward orgasm.

A MAN'S FEAR

Phil, when you had vibrations in your pelvis you became frightened. Well, now it's for you to decide whether you want to remain scared of those feelings or whether you want to learn to enjoy them. If you go on conditioning yourself to be alive in a limited or exclusive way, if you insist that certain conditions be met, you'll deaden your world and go around with a sense of suffering.

Your heaviness, especially the puffiness from the waist down, reveals your need to hold back and not move, to deaden sensations in that area and create a kind of sexual frigidity. A lot of warm feelings move out from the upper part of your body but you inhibit them from the waist down.

Phil: When feelings began to come through my pelvis, I panicked. I was scared of my sexual feelings. I withdrew from them.

In working my feelings through I discovered that I had been deadening myself to avoid my father's wrath. I was living my father's puritanism. I don't have to acquiesce to my father. My feelings don't have to be his.

Stan: You're beginning to be free to be independent or satisfied. You let yourself lose control when you screamed "Daddy!" I hope that same loss of control can allow you to have an erection. At one time you may have been afraid to have erections or penis feelings around your father. But now if loss of control means having an erection—let it. There's no father to punish you any more.

DECONDITIONING

Clara: "The feeling that I had from my mother was: "That which is pleasurable is evil." I don't believe it any more intellectually, but my body still responds as if I do.

Stan: The head gets conditioned along with the rest of the body; then you decondition the head but the conditioning is still there in the muscular structure. You've only deconditioned one circuit, and the other circuit is still active. So the head is free, but the feelings are the same as they were in the past because of how we structured them in the body. Working with the body's rigidities helps decondition our brains, our feelings and our muscles.

Working With Groups

WHAT ONE FINDS in the family one finds in social groups. A group is also a living entity composed of many individual members connected in a certain fashion. Every group has a character, a way of moving and expressing itself.

Groups make people more individualistic or suppress them. They support emotional and bodily life or they deny it. Some groups nourish the empathy that grows out of holding and touching oneself and the bodies of others. Some groups teach the denial of one's body and others' bodies; they teach distancing from touching and being touched, and this creates observers, people who keep the world at arm's length.

Working in a group encourages us to share our bodiliness—I don't mean in nude-athons or group orgies or touchy-feely ways, but through looking at our physicalness and learning to feel its expression in ourselves and in others; learning to again be erotic in the sense of having feeling, having reason with feeling.

When I work with groups it's no different from a one-to-one situation. In a one-to-one situation I view the person as a living process. I try to perceive how he resists movement and feeling, how he expresses his needs, how he lives his body, and what his body says about how he is alive.

I approach a group not only to see its personal characteristics, but also to see if there is the possibility of generating the soup of feeling that either encourages or discourages a bodily life. Can there be an eroticizing without words, without resorting to pornography or obscene body techniques? I don't make use of mechanical gymnastics or exercises, but rather natural movements—like reaching out or letting the chest down or shaking the pelvis—to create a feeling atmosphere in which everyone in the room may participate in their own way, inwardly or publicly.

Of course, the experience of the leader, as well as his philosophical stance, helps determine the direction the group takes. But, more important, the feelings the leader has and the emotional life he leads become the hallmarks from which people learn about their own bodily aliveness. When the leader is emotionally healthy, the members of the group can take cues from him to learn about their own bodily responses without fear of being humiliated or misused, without fear of behaving in a way they might later regret.

When I work with a person while others are in an observer's role, the intensity of the person's reactions, the quality of energy released, and the dynamics of his experience transform the others from observers to empathizers. The empathizers become participants in this drama of a person's allowing his own energetic feeling process to emerge as actions and sounds, talking and dancing.

This is a crucial transformation. Our observer role creates distance. To permit our emotional involvement, to let ourselves be touched by events in the group experience, helps develop an empathizing function and a critical faculty that does not depend on aloofness and distance. The transforming of our observer role begins to re-eroticize us, doing away with those alienating attitudes that make us seem foreign to our bodies and to others. This allows us to identify with feelings and to trust our bodily responses again.

Chronic muscle contraction prevents feeling and movement. When the chronic spasms of someone's bodily and emotional set begin to be more motile, the radiation of feeling and emotion affects others in such a way that all become connected without verbal communication. We have all experienced how a high point in a sports event sends a wave of excitement or gloom through a crowd. This radiation of feeling is an energetic phenomenon that group members begin to experience.

When I'm working with a person in a group, I usually notice that the rest of the group first becomes involved by sharing the responses that are generated by the person working. The sharing puts the group members in touch with their own responses, which in turn generates supportive feedback for the person I'm working with. This energetic exchange brings about a field of organismic empathy; the empathy is transmitted like a water current, originating with the movements and feelings, gestures and expressions of the active member of the group.

The process seems to follow a sequence. Everybody's excitement builds, then they experience inhibitions to their build-up, then they work through the inhibition by insight or by letting their tensions melt. This process leads to feeling, to the development of more free excitation manifesting a higher level of vibration, which encourages new perceptions and responses to self, to others, and to place.

Our families and social groups frown upon our being publicly bodily and emotionally expressive, and also of being privately sensuous. So, to win approval, we adopt attitudes of pride, roles, and ideals that deny our bodies. It makes no difference that these attitudes don't suit us, that they keep us searching for satisfaction that eludes. We settle for group praise and applause. In this way our families and peer groups have taught us to deaden our feelings, such as excitement in the genitals and impulses to touch. We are punished when we reach out to touch "improperly," so we learn to imitate the stiffness of those around us. An excited response to another person's beauty is forbidden, so we turn our excitement into pedestal worship. Properness and calm resignation are indicative of English and American queues—as opposed to the noisy explosiveness and laughter that mark the queues in Italy.

When our social group is restrictive, we develop all sorts of fantasies. We call up pictures of what we want and we plan ways to get it. We ward off spontaneous impulses and substitute others. We try to be "good" so we can be loved. We do what is right or sanctioned, and in this way we perpetuate the common body stances and action patterns of our society.

Somebody working in the presence of a group is like somebody growing up in a certain society. I work with one person, and the others share the experience in a supportive or antagonistic way. As the person lives through the process of softening his rigidities and repossessing his feelings, the whole group becomes involved, learning about their own tightnesses and emotional stiffnesses.

I have also worked with groups in which everybody's involvement has been more direct, where everyone has participated in the work that aids grounding and the emotional expression that increases pleasure. Sometimes this consists of working in a circle, holding hands and touching feet, sitting up or lying down. I have had groups try, while following their breathing, to locate sensations flowing downward toward the ground. I have had groups do some of the basic bioenergetic movements designed to get people into contact with the ground by letting excitement into their hindlegs and feet; they can then open their resistances to feelings by feeling their physical restrictions to movement and by recognizing that their pain is really a silent, fearful protest. They may first articulate this protest—this NO—in an infantile way, such as screaming, kicking, or tantrums; and then by more focused kicking and hitting (aimed at a bed), or by looking others in the eye and saying "no" while noticing the feelings going through their bodies to the earth and to the other. Later I encourage motions of softly reaching out, moving toward others and away, so that they may experience connection and separation.

When a group of people are sitting in a circle there is generally a flow of feeling—from the abdomen to the feet to the floor—and a sharing of breathing flame, so to speak. There is sensation in the hands, forming a feeling of no-separation. In the sitting and lying positions there are many channels of communication. If one of the group is feeling no connection, other members send out streamers of excitement to connect to him, to help him be part of the group feeling. Patterns of crisscrossing feeling may occur if there is a particular person who will not or cannot join the group; the empty space is bridged by the energy of the people on either side jumping over it, thus making a smaller circle. Connections come about by affinity and approval. One can still retain his freedom and privacy and not be bullied into a group event.

These energetic events are not always seen, but they are subjectively perceived and described. The charge in a room after a period of time can be tremendous. We then realize we are all connected nonverbally to ourselves, to others, to nature. The quality of this nonverbal bodily talk turns out to be satisfying, pleasurable. We participate without ever having to lose our individuality. We all share the same life-giving environment.

Man is a living organism. We develop individuality; but we have in common the fact that we are all bodies, bodies that have grown in unique ways. We desire to share, to participate, but we don't always know how. When this occurs we feel distance, suspicion and hate.

The group acts as an energy generator and as a transformer of feelings. When I am working with one person, I count on the other group members to contribute energy to a situation. They intensify whatever feeling is in the room, amplifying it so that the feelings and psychological responses of the person working press for more expression—which in turn calls forth still more group participation. This is why there is more involvement in a group than in a one-to-one arrangement; a group steps up the intensity of what is happening and helps satisfaction occur. A one-to-one situation doesn't have to be less intense. It can be very intense in its way; it is often more private than a group experience. But the more private nature of the one-to-one situation may only involve the verbal information that a person is willing to transmit. A person in a one-to-one situation is likely to transmit more deeply personal fantasies, wishes, or difficulties than he will in a group. But this apparent depth of involvement can be an illusion. In a group, although a deep involve-

ment may be unspoken and therefore generally unrec-
ognized, it can occur nonverbally as physical, emotional expression (or lack of it) and is open for
everyone to see and respond to. There is no hiding the
heavy breathing of fear or excitement. There is no
hiding the seductive movements of one's pelvis when
one is aroused. When we let ourselves respond to
these signs, our bodies change and our insides talk to
us as well as to others with approval or disapproval.
We become more expressive or more tight. We maintain our stance or we change.

A person always expresses a quantity and a quality of feeling. Never is there no feeling. If a person
refuses to express himself overtly, the effort involved
in refusing is in itself an expression, which is picked
up by the whole group. Stasis, withdrawal out of fear
or spite, is an action which requires energy—possibly
more energy than movement, for one is putting out
both the energy of movement and the energy committed to arrest this movement. A person's continuum of
activity is expressive, whether it communicates expansion, contraction, or containment.

Being eroticized, becoming a more feeling bodily
person, involves more than just an increase in pleasure
and vitality. If a person feels hate or shame and stays
with that feeling, he too becomes erotic. Feelings accepted and contained bodily are what make us erotic,
more alive somatically, be they of love or hate. It is up
to us to make life livable.

A group can often transform negative feeling
—take out its toxic effect—when the members main-

tain a high motile process, a running ocean of feeling which dilutes the poison. But groups may also turn sour and hostile and enhance the negativity. Again, the depth of the leader's own goodness of feeling and his own ability to maintain a high level of excitement can act like the north star. His life feeling points the way.

When I work with a group—one at a time or everyone together—I attempt to contact the stoppages in process. Then I encourage movement and feeling, which creates an expansive thrust that tends to weaken inhibitions by generating pleasure instead of the pain of cramping.

In a typical group, not only do we attempt to locate the muscular cramps that hold us off the ground and limit our sensations, we also learn the physicality of the roles we assume—how we play Big Brother by making our feet and faces immobile, how we play Big Sister by being soft and sympathetic. The work we do encourages the emergence of the unexpected, such as the automatic movement of the pelvis, or the spontaneous, non-self-conscious move to touch or cry. Unlike most other groups I have witnessed, we don't need much verbal confrontation. We don't verbally attack defenses, role-playing, or games. I am not putting down these practices, but in our breathing, in our gestures and expressive feelings, we communicate our quality of biological aliveness all the time, and verbal explanation is unnecessary—although the appropriate language of expression may include words.

Think of a flock of birds on a telephone wire. One

bird rises and flies away and every other bird instantly follows suit. It is the establishment of this kind of communication that makes the difference between satisfaction and dissatisfaction.

With the groups I've worked with, my experience has been that after two or three days everyone develops a feeling of awe and respect for what the human being is bodily. The group generates deeply respectful and even religious attitudes toward life and the body. It generates an understanding of other people, and a feeling of connectedness. I've never yet failed to see this happen. As the group goes on, people get more and more in touch with what they're feeling and what other people's bodies are expressing, more and more able to identify bodily inhibitions and spasms, to recognize the language of emotional expression, to feel the process of how they and others gain satisfaction.

In the same way that an impulse starts in one part of the body and comes to the foreground to gain attention and satisfaction, so each group member stepping up to express himself moves out of the background to receive the attention and support of the group as well as that of the individual. The group encourages or discourages patterns of physicalness, encourages or discourages the way a person uses his body with the group and for himself.

A group is either supportive of bodily life or it is not. A group cannot be pro-life when it is not pro-body. The ground of living is the realm of biological process. Our soul is the communal expression of our cellular history and our cellular present. To be alive is to be an animal—what kind of animal depends upon our family and, by extension, our social group. The kinds of satisfactions that we learn make us friends or enemies of our bodies and others' bodies.

In my work, I aim to enable a person to be more pleasurable, to live this process, to tolerate a higher level of energy and experience the feeling and vision which are some of its concomitants. When a person is more energetic, more of himself, he has more freedom to be part of a group—not as a submitter but as an active member. Being able to express himself gives the person more choice to connect with others.

Doris was a twenty-five year old woman who worked with me in a group setting. She told me that she had no orgasm, was always submissive to authorities, and had a job she couldn't stand. She never complained; she held back her angry feelings. She had a self-defeating attitude toward life, a puppet-like quality that could be described as that of the "nice girl." This was the role she used to contact others—her social role—for which she expected approval. She had little ability to assert herself or to be alone and see frustrating situations through to their conclusion.

When Doris presented herself in the workshop she revealed a rigid immobility: the front of her body was as taut as a drumhead, and her spine was very stiff and straight. She hardly moved. It was as if all her life were funneled up to her shiny eyes. There was a conservative deadenedness in her face, even though she smiled a lot. I could plainly see the relationship between the "nice girl" role, which she created by deadening and stiffening her body, and her resulting inability to assert herself, to express her feelings and have orgastic pleasure. She had a lot of shyness about her body and her feelings. At first the group responded to her sympathetically, but her continuous struggles with shame and unresponsiveness provoked irritation. Some of the others discussed their own feelings of shame about their bodies and told how they were shamed as a way of disciplining.

The first time Doris worked she was like an immovable stone; even group urging did not change this unyieldingness. She worked for an hour trying to mobilize some expression of protest, trying to say "no." She was unable to say "no" with any conviction or energy. All her protests were flat. She kicked like a little robot—mechanically, on command—but nothing could incite her, move her. There was hardly an instant of aliveness in the entire session. Her aloofness was saying, "I won't be shamed by anyone again, so stay away," and the group felt this rejection. However, she did recognize her inability to say "no" directly, and she saw that the frozenness which did it for her was the link to her problems.

The next time we worked she aroused the entire group's irritation by way of her immobility, her body that said "no." This group antagonism, which was a reply to her bodily rejection of people, moved her to cry. The group had the effect of intensifying her feelings of loneliness—so much so that she began to cry and thus to soften her physical and emotional hardness. But then she got angry with this display of "weakness."

Later I asked Doris to breathe heavily, to create an expansive situation in the front of her body by strong inhalation and strong exhalation. After she started to breathe there began to be some movement in her chest. She reported that little ripples of sensation were beginning to emerge, and she told us that her breasts were becoming more pleasurable, that there was a general spreading of feeling throughout her body. She began to soften and all of a sudden she began to cry again. She had a great deal of difficulty with this because she felt that crying humiliated her. Along with her, many members of the group felt their own repressed crying, and their own rage as they somatically recalled their shame. They felt how, like Doris, they withheld their crying by stiffening their upper lips. They felt how they squelched their anger by clasping their throats and hands.

As the sensations continued to move through Doris we observed a spastic ring around her pelvis. The ring inhibited the flow downward and changed her crying to a mood of disgust. She said she wanted to vomit. I encouraged her to do this. Then she said that she had always felt disgusted and shamed.
her parents did not like her body and had shamed her for needing tenderness and touching. They would punish her by making fun of her, by ridiculing her. Later, she associated sexual feelings with this same disgust because they provoked the urge to touch her-

self, the need and the desire to touch others. To need others brought shame; it was something to dislike. Her self-dislike made her socially submissive. It also made her an accessible sexual object for others because, here again, she would submit. Meanwhile she felt betrayed. She also felt inwardly rebellious against her female-ness because she had taken on the sexual role of pleasing without wanting. Her inner rebelliousness screamed at the group, "I dislike myself! I dislike you!" With the disgust came rage. She began to make biting and tearing movements with her mouth. She wanted to rip everything apart.

After this rage Doris became very quiet, but not quiet in her usual, dead way. Her softness now sup-ported a fuller breathing. She began to experience very pleasurable and tender feelings throughout her whole body, and she began to feel her femaleness. She began to feel that her bodily sensations could and did give pleasure. She felt entitled to live out these soft, quiet feelings. At the same time all of us in the group had individually been through a symphony of our own memories of self-dislike. As we began to sigh and breathe deeper, our own soft feelings became a warm bath of approval for Doris. She led us to it; we shared her process.

You need only imagine the reverse of this process to see the levels of what Doris experienced. As a girl, she felt the softness that is natural to everybody. On the next level, she moved into a profound rage that this soft feeling was being interfered with. The level above that was her anxiety and disgust for what she was feeling; the next was crying over her hopelessness. Next came her immobility and finally the casting of the social actress, "the good girl." She joined the group because the pleasure of this role no longer sufficed. She wanted direct body satisfaction.

After going through her group experience, she felt an aliveness in just walking, in being present—even in being by herself, which she had always hated before. She was more connected to her own feelings. She had her own life to nourish now. Her protests had meaning and necessity.

Her emotional strait jacket served the function of forcing her into a state of submissiveness and immobility without commitment to her body. Because she was not able to contact herself, she could not be alone and was compulsively driven to find some kind of company outside herself. The loosening of her emotional and muscular armour reconnected her with herself and others and helped her regain her sense of self-pleasure. All this was supported by the group, each of whom also had a stake in participating in a process meant to provide a base for contact, a uterus for responsiveness. As a consequence, Doris experienced that she now had the ability to defend herself. No longer did she merely accept and tolerate the deadening influence of the cultural milieu in which she grew up. And she learned that others could feel with her, not against her—others who, rather than saying, "we love you but reject your body," said, "we can accept your feelings and your body without your being a girl."

Doris is a good example of how we form acceptable images—e.g., the "nice girl"—restricting ourselves
to minimal contact, negating aliveness for acceptance,
so that we may remain in some kind of connection to
others. After all, being connected to a group by being
distant is better than being exiled. We must all be part
of a group or we do not survive long; we suffer
emotional torture. This is why we submit to group
pressure to deny our bodies.

Both conceptually and in practice, the rooting of a
person in the body—in one's sexuality, in one's sensu-
ousness, in one's feelings and sensations—is deeply
pleasurable. It is the natural bond of groups and
families. Without it, we form bonds that are painful.

A man who was in one of my workshops wrote
me this note: "I have just returned from what, in my
personal point of view, were the most remarkable
three weeks of my adult life. I deeply experienced two
bioenergetic workshops, one at Esalen and the other
at Lake Tahoe. They *flowed* and *pulsated*, like nothing
else I have experienced, and somehow they flowed
and pulsated through *me*. I didn't do them—I just let
them happen. After all the work, and all the learning,
all the fears and doubts about myself, it was as though
a fresh spring, which had been bubbling slowly
stronger . . . suddenly opened up and I *flowed*. What
made it especially great was that my son Larry was
with me all of the time and took part in the workshops. He was fine and it was great to get to know
each other . . ."

EMOTIONAL
SURVIVAL

Culture and Disease

WHAT INTERESTS ME is a person's feeling, form and expression and how that person relates to his environment. In any society this relationship is forced into certain channels. The culture tells people what behavior patterns are acceptable and punishes deviations. All social forms—work patterns, marriages and sexual contracts, ways of raising and educating our kids—ritualize behavior. And the ritualizing of behavior has its consequences. People are beginning to see that this culture we've created produces much of the sickness we're faced with. Our community, our society, is the background for many specific illnesses.

I had a practice in a poor section of New York and got one class of people, and another practice on Central Park West and got a different clientele. Yet in both locations I found a common factor: the inability to live a bodily life in this culture.

Wilhelm Reich claimed that many diseases are the result of damming up one's sexual energy. Hans Selye has said very much the same thing. He calls it the stress syndrome. Basically, he's saying that every disease process is the same in its beginning phase: there's a general alarm reaction that constitutes the first line of defense—an energetic flush, along with an overall step-up in the metabolism. If the organism cannot respond there is collapse, and death occurs as the result of exhaustion.

There have been research projects in connection with the above. One project had to do with heart disease being related to changes in life style. Major heart attacks took place at times when the people under study were going through a great deal of crisis. There was stress and challenge that these people were unwilling and unable to meet. Their organisms would not expand.

People under a long siege of muscular contraction, of self-discipline, of holding tight, cannot suddenly be flexible. If people have lost their plasticity, their ability to expand, if they cannot respond to an expansive force even when it's pleasurable, then they generally suffer a blowout—or degeneration.

A research project at Stanford showed that a condition of chronic despair and loneliness provides a fertile ground for cancer. The cancer can then be triggered by a particular stress. Reich also speculated that cancer was related to resignation. He said that a

person unable to have a gratifying instinctual life de-
spairs and resigns, and this resignation creates the
background for cancer. Everybody called him a nut.
René DuBois says that cancer is a social disease, in the
same way that tuberculosis epidemics were related to
the sweat-shop era.

I believe it's true that cancer is a social disease.
The kinds of stresses that we encounter in our culture
result in a particular kind of exhaustion. We intention-
ally encourage alienation by postulating that competi-
tiveness and high achievement are signs of potency.
But there can only be so many winners. And even if
they do achieve, it often turns out to be unfulfilling. A
person winds up despairing and then may be on the
road to cancer.

It is important to see how we interfere with our
normal organismic processes. This interference generates life forms which are not inherently self-regulating.
Many of us are so committed to social ideals that we
prohibit the development of our instinctual lives. Our
commitment to the outside world effectively separates
us from the life processes of our biological selves.

I found this out when I studied protoplasm. I
realized that the functions we possess on our high
level of human organization already exist in protoplasm. Cellular protoplasm exhibits all the qualities
and functions of the human organism: contracting,
expanding, containing, remembering, deciding, discharging, and so on. We are the unfolding, the further
specialization, of the already specialized life processes
called protoplasm. If a person is connected with his

basic biological state, all the qualities of humanness will naturally emerge.

Slowing down a person's processes creates structure. Speeding up a person's processes destroys structure. If we want somebody to be stable and predictable, we restrict the streaming of his excitation. Conversely, if we want him to be more labile, more precocious, we step up his bodily processes. What we call structure is not static, it's really slow process —which is another way of saying that one's body expresses the process of one's life. The attempts one makes to control, alter, or misuse one's structure lead for the most part to disease.

The limitation of many psychotherapies is directly related to their inability to go beyond insight to change the processes which generate bodily structure. Group interactivity is now attempting to change process by encouraging personal action and an awareness of interpersonal dynamics, but none of these psychotherapies aims at changing body structure in order to foster growth.

In the work I do, the relationship between form and the expanding-contracting processes is quite evident. The structure of a self-defeating person is usually muscle-bound. When he begins to expand, he comes up against the culturally reinforced rigidities that he has created in his body. He experiences struggle and a sense of fruitlessness. There is pressure toward expansive self-affirmation, and then suddenly there's inhibition; he can't find a way out of his physical and emotional imprisonment.

The structure of a person who lives a compressed life is taut, physically indrawn. This sort of structure begins in an environment that is conducive to withdrawal: the hospital. We've created birth conditions in the hospitals that would make any life want to withdraw. It's ridiculous! Here's a kid who's been living in an environment of 98.6 degrees, in close harmony with the mother. After all this closeness the natural thing would be for the child to enter the world and to be cleaned and held by the mother, held for long periods of time until it can wean itself away toward independence. The natural thing would be to maintain a continuity between the inside of the uterus and the outside of the mother's body, so that contact with the outer world is not a shock of sudden alienation that lays in patterns of fear.

But we don't let the child be with the mother. Instead, we pull it out and stick it in a sterile room. Then we give the mother a schedule: she can see the baby only at certain hours. The baby's environment immediately becomes less life-supportive. Who wouldn't protest or withdraw? Hospital behavior is inhuman, yet we accept it. And our acceptance has the effect of perpetuating our basic cultural statement that to want physical contact is "bad."

Lousy mothers and schizophrenia go together. Harry Harlow proved that with his monkeys. Doesn't this affirm the relationship between the culture we've created and the disease we've created?

Just imagine for a moment a woman with a tightly contracted womb, a woman who has difficulty having feeling. Imagine the womb of that woman being the farmland for a growing seed of life. What kind of child will emerge from that contracted space? And then think of this in terms of the cultural state we've set up. What kinds of individuals grow out of it?

The capacity to expand and contract ties in with the ability to make choices. If our expanding, contactful process comes to a place where the expanding can't continue, either we're going to de-structure our ideals and permit the processes of our tissue to occur, or we're not. We have that choice.

We can recover our bodily life. We can learn to regulate our life-style according to our bodily processes. In so doing, we can create a new cultural form. Or we can go on being long-faced animals.

Death and Survival

IF YOU THINK BIOLOGICALLY instead of technologically, you're going to end up with a different world-view. Einstein talked about the importance of the observer in relation to the event observed. It turned me on to this: living is relationship; living is relativistic. How we relate to our own nature determines how we perceive the rest of our world. If we are instinctually inhibited or immature, then our observations will reflect that.

This left me with trying to learn from the integrity of my own processes, so that I could understand what my truth is. And I came to understand that the more alive I am, the more I know my truth. The life of me *is* my truth. The more I perceive myself, the less I have to debate about the nature of truth. Much becomes self-evident in the process of living. The more I get my consciousness out of my head and into the rest of me, the more of me experiences my truth. And when I look at my culture from this place, from the truth of my own biological existence, I see things a little differently.

Our technical advances seem to have been made at the price of biological sacrifices, starting with the pleasure zones, and I take offense at that. The question is this: is the price we pay for our enculturation worth it? When I have to pay with my gut, in literal terms like needing to have it removed, I think that's too big a price. Am I really willing to participate in a culture that encourages me to give up the use of my legs so that I can have the privilege of driving a car with an automatic transmission?

Let's put it this way: since I'm alive now, I'd like to be oriented to what my life is now. For centuries we have existed for tomorrow. The "tomorrow" game is epitomized by our industrial world. Methods of child-rearing, especially toilet-training, produce the concepts of regularity, productivity, and predictability —the philosophy of "on time" and "later." Both diarrhea and constipation are bad, but diarrhea is worse. In school we learn to wait for the break and to finish in a hurry, and always to make, to produce, perform.

We usually assume that delayed gratification is worth it. That's the mainstay of our civilization. But in making that assumption we weaken our contact with pleasure. There is nothing wrong with planning and building for the future, but when futurizing becomes the goal of existence our lives grow lopsided.

Deep chronic muscular contractions alter your perceptual ground, leading either to conservatism or to a desperate, explosive desire for revolution. But there is another impulse which asks: are you willing to be a metabolic fire, to be a burning life which relentlessly consumes old structures and illuminates new form? Can you be in love with living?

If you watch the way I conduct my work, you know that the idea is to get you to experience for yourself that movement is more pleasurable than chronic contraction; to demonstrate to yourself that the pleasure you get from being contracted and inhibited—the pleasure that you get from that rigid kind of security—is far less satisfying than the pleasure of moving and being vital. But if you accept your internal flow, you also accept the fact of your impending death. That's something that most of us don't want to deal with. Because we are afraid of our dying process we try to preserve life at any cost.

People who are dying are never asked if they are willing to die. Their "helpers" assume that they must live. Why the hell can't we let people die? When you get into a place where you're not thinking *from* life but *about* life, you wind up doing crazy things. The attempts to preserve life at any cost fill our institutions with more crippled children than you can imagine and turn older people into plumbing factories. Statistics show an increase in life, but they never talk about the quality of life.

Years ago, a teacher of mine was talking about the

nervous system and demonstrating some reaction or other. And then he said: "Kids, just remember that the living force takes your life, just as much as it supports your life, and you'd better get that into your heads." That is true. Life lives you and kills you.

The most consistent experience I have of life is that there is pattern and form. Life is anything but patternless. From living I have reverence for life's pattern. I also have the understanding that life is bigger than my ego, bigger than anything my ego could ever comprehend. I relate to that with appreciation and awe.

With the Eskimo, for instance, when a person is no longer useful he goes out onto the ice and sits down and dies. That really makes sense, provided you don't see death as horrible. But the reason you see death as something horrible is that you are not immersed in your present living. A person who is contactfully immersed is less afraid to die. Somebody who has an unlived life resents dying.

Every deep-seated muscular contraction tries to preserve a sense of wholeness by cultivating a sense of hope, by futurizing and extending time. Every deep-seated contraction impedes the flow of excitation, slows metabolic processes and creates a relatively static condition. The fantasy that arises out of this is: "I have slowed the flow of time; I am eternal."

These contractions don't allow us to die properly. They restrict our ability to participate with our dying insofar as we're conditioned to hold on, conditioned to inhibit flow and expression.

We have the right to object to our dying, but we can't just deny it. In Bergman's *Seventh Seal*, in the last part, the messenger of death comes, and the characters are giving him their "I don't want to die," and "be merciful" routine. And one guy in that whole group says: "Okay, you've come to get me and take away my life, and I protest—I'm not going without protest." Or Dylan Thomas: "Do not go gentle into that good night. Rage, rage against the dying of the light."

But neither Bergman's nor Thomas' protest is a denial of the experience. What we do is to accept the *fact* of death but deny ourselves the *experience* of dying.

Contractions stop time. They deny experiencing. They make process dense, static. Then we interpret this static structure as survival, first in relationship to a particular situation, and then we extend it into many situations. From a contracted state, we cannot perceive a dynamic universe.

What do we expect during an increased life span? Do we want to preserve the world we know? Man is an agent of change. All life generates change.

There is constant encounter with the emotions of change. This makes us realize that change is deeper than social forms; it is explicit in the energetic processes of man and the world. It is innovativeness versus tradition.

Our increased life span demands that we engage in processes of change, even though today's leaders think that to go with the new will kill them. All was well when we were able to leave change to the ages—when, if we were lucky, we lived to 40. Now we live to 68 or 75. We didn't have so many opportunities for change then; we do now. Technology has caught up somewhat with our dreams of evolving our relationship with the world. We can actualize some of our dreams. Traditional life styles don't work any more. The world is changing too fast and we're living longer. Our political, economic, and marital systems are not built for long-term, seventy-year lives.

This is our dilemma, individually and collectively—that the new creates endless possibilities while longevity tends to want to preserve what is.

The revolution/evolution we are experiencing today is a demand for reconnection with our bodies. Coming to an end is our acceptance of the promise of reward, pleasure, satisfaction *tomorrow*.

Crumbling, I hope, going, I hope, are the attitudes that separate feeling from action: be orderly, be predictable, sit still, be nice, stand straight, be proper, hold back, be perfect, be monogamous—the emphasis on self-tailoring rather than on self-expanding. These attitudes are based on contractedness, compressedness, rather than on a contained expandedness.

In short, we're beginning to want our bodies back. And yet we're simultaneously afraid to have them back and ignorant of how to get them back.

How did we give up our bodies in the first place? The loss of our bodies, as I see it, has two roots, both of them originating in the process of civilizing ourselves. One is our attempt to live up to images of what to be, images we've created to win approval and to meet our fundamental needs. Be a clown to avoid rejection and get attention. Be a scientist, cold and doubting, to be admired and to be of service to society. Be shy and sensitive in order to avoid conflict. Be obedient and well-behaved in order to be praised. Be a space man. Be a sexpot—and so on, ad infinitum. We have given up the right to project our own images of how we want to be, the right to be what we feel and experience now.

The second root of our trying to disconnect from our bodies is our attempt to overcome the pain of our finiteness and the helplessness of our dying. We have done this by "spiritualizing" ourselves, by invoking other dimensions of existence and investing them with more value than this existence. Both spiritualizing and the setting up of images teach us, directly or indirectly, to live for the future.

The lived body is an expression of the historical past, the reality of here and now, and the emerging tomorrow. The living body gestates its own time and space. Man is a bodied being, and his sexuality is the link between himself and others.

All would agree that sexuality should be pleasurable. Yet contracted muscle states are testimony to our wanting to inhibit our sexual pleasure. Self-contractions lead to a *conceptual* connection with the world instead of a sensual-sexual connection. They substitute conceptualized experience for the direct experience of pleasure.

At one time my "goodness" supposedly came from the purity of my thoughts and deeds rather than from the bodily pleasure I got out of doing things. Sexual love was the devil. We can now perceive that physical doing and being are at least as pleasurable as the cold satisfaction of living up to an idea. The body is joyful. Its joy is poetry. Can there be pleasure without love? Can there be love without physical pleasure? The heart warms the entire bodily self.

Pleasure is that feeling which is truthful to one's becoming. Sadness can be pleasurable; conflict can be pleasurable. Pleasure expands the imagination.

Pleasure does not come about merely by avoiding pain or by achieving hedonistic goals. It arises from contact, self-expression, self-revelation.

The return to a pleasurable body is a goal of oldsters. The young are born innately capable of pleasure and need simply be encouraged to live it. We're starting to recognize that most of our chronic attitudes and muscular contractions are designed to prevent biological pleasure and to supplant it with non-biological satisfaction. We don't regain our sensuality by heightening our sensory awareness, but by immersing ourselves in our streamings. The concept of pleasure *versus* pain holds true only if we deny that the whole is bigger than the sum of its parts. The sum of me knows pleasure and pain. The whole of me encompasses my pain and makes it part of my life, which is a good life. Pleasurable feelings don't consist of the absence of pain. They're the natural outgrowth of being alive. All mystics report that the enlightened states are pleasurable and sexual.

We who think that we are gods because we have created a world are in our own trap. We try to enjoy that which we have created, instead of enjoying the creator in the act of creation.

Evolution:
A Participatory
Cosmology

IN LIVING THE LIFE OF THE BODY there is a continuing development, a growing and evolving of one's self and one's world.

There is a tendency in this day and age to pathologize everybody and then to therapize them. I feel too vital in my own being to accept this tendency. Therapy is not life. And I'm not talking as a therapist. I'm talking as an intuitive thinker and as an artist.

I see myself as an energetic process, part of an evolutionary force. When I'm able to perceive myself in this way, the phenomena I see around me cease to take on a doomsday quality. One can be concerned with changing and growing without confusing destruction for destructuring, or revolution for evolution.

I believe that we are in the middle of an evolutionary thrust that is as deep as anything mankind has experienced in historical time. I experience it in me as a pulsatory wave, an open-ended expanding and contracting, a rhythm of excitement and form. Evolution has its ups and downs, peaking and troughing from old to new boundaries.

I feel that our age is changing. We are peaking now, moving out toward new limits, new definitions, new borders. There's a tremendous amount of activity, with concomitant anxieties and excited desires for new form and pleasure—all the signs of a high-energy state. Every high-energy state, of necessity, destructures its old forms and builds new ones.

This is the broad background I tie myself into with the work that I do. I work with what is fundamentally, innately growing. I want to bring that to the front.

The people I work with have bodies that commonly reveal weakness, collapse, compressed excitement, puffiness, flabbiness, immaturity, rigidity, and hardness. They have inflexible faces, spines that don't bend and skin that doesn't wrinkle. But these people are generally between 25 and 45, what I call the industrial age set. When I look at the younger people —sixteen, fifteen, fourteen—I get a different picture. These young people are living in a time of enormous crisis. And we can't define people who are living in crisis. We can't describe crisis in terms of pathology. What's to be expected of young people who are the avant-garde of our biological evolution? We may be witnessing a new breed of human being.

If I can help people experience their basic pulsatory rhythms, they become capable of vitalizing themselves, of tapping into something which is them and bigger than them. What emerges doesn't fit any model that I know.

Let me give you an example. One time I was working with a man who was expressing his protest by kicking very strongly, breathing very strongly, and all of a sudden he stopped. He stopped kicking and he even stopped breathing. I thought he was dead, and I said, "Bill, Bill!" Nothing happened. I said it again. Then he stirred, opened his eyes and said, "Oh, I'm okay, but I was concerned about your concern so I came back."

"What are you talking about?" I asked him. "What happened, where were you?"

"I was in a pleasurable place, a magnificent place."

I had thought he was dead. And I said to myself, "Oh, he split out. He dissociated from himself and then froze up." That's what went through me.

But then he started to tell me more. He told me what he had learned about himself and what he had connected with: deep pleasure and a flow of inner events which freed him from his habitual attitudes. He told me that he directly grasped the origin of his rigidities and the part they played in restricting this flow. And it dawned on me that Bill was describing a *pause* state, a transitional state. He was in that place in his pulsatory rhythm where he was experiencing a pause—inhalation–pause–exhalation–pause–inhalation—that global place of transition where the unformed emerges into form. I say this emphatically because, when he did come back, he knew a lot about himself, and from that point on he really began to take charge of his life. He perceived the crazy situation he was in at home and at work, and he began to change it. He began to tell me what was going on; I didn't need to tell him. It was a revelation to me. And I pulled back and said to myself, "Stanley Keleman, you're a lucky dog you didn't stick to a dogmatic idea of what was happening."

There is a space in which the new emerges. How can we begin to look at that? How can we begin to use that?

Many people I come in contact with have had an experience similar to Bill's. They recognize it the minute I bring their attention to it. The pause is the expression of a person disengaging from his present structure, touching his roots.

And I began to ask myself this: what would happen if I didn't interfere with somebody's pause state, if I demanded nothing and allowed that person's existential qualities to emerge, his own rhythms, his own patterns of charging and discharging? What if I allowed him to "speak up," didn't push too hard for a build-up or a release of his excitement?

In Bill's case his excitement began to suffuse him with feeling-information that became feeling-communication. It connected him with others and himself. It changed the nature of the relationship that I had with him and he with me.

As I watched this process develop in Bill and as I watched him stand up again, I saw what may be a natural law at work. For me, it's become an important principle. From the pause between contracting and expanding comes the excitement that lifts man to his feet.

Life, in its expanding, invades new dimensions. It thrusts itself from the sea onto the land. It thrusts man from crawling to standing. It thrusts man from being in his environment to encountering his environment. It thrusts the baby from the womb. It thrusts man forward into his mysterious future. Life, in its abundance, projects itself into the unknown of new potentialities.

Our standing up is a charge that takes us from the horizontal position to the vertical position. An increase in the amplitude of our pulsatory wave moves us from the horizontal world to the vertical world. The vertical position which makes us unique is itself the direct expression of our evolution.

Uprightness has inherent in it the forming of new relationships. To be vertical is to be unstable. It's an unsure position. One remains standing by keeping oneself from falling down.

We fluctuate between horizontality and verticality. Our verticality is not stable and maybe it never will be, because life is an oscillating process. We go to sleep and we wake up. We lie down and we stand up. And in that standing up, in which we rise out of the horizontal animal world, a gigantic thing happens. We become *human* animals. Because of the higher charge granted to us—if I can put it that way—we find ourselves uniquely related to nature.

The upright position is itself an expression of changing relationship. We are the only animals who can form relationships spontaneously and artificially. We don't have a stabilized instinctual system which determines and fixes our behavior. We're open-ended, which permits us a great measure of novelty and experimentation; we engage in more selection than horizontality permits us.

An animal in the horizontal position does not have its soft parts exposed. When a man stands he faces others, open to the world, his soft parts vulnerable. Not his head and eyes alone, but his throat, his chest, his abdomen, his genitals. This ventral exposure gives rise to new contact. To walk one step at a time and to see into the distance leads to the measurement of space—the birth of mathematics and geometry.

Man's verticality, his unique relationship with nature, has enabled him to explore and innovate, to build his world, his civilization. Civilization is the production of nature working through man.

When I work with people I ask them to lie down and experience the relative helplessness of horizontality. Then I ask them to stand again and re-experience the excitement which makes them unique human animals. The instability of verticality is not a problem; the fundamental truth about verticality is that it *is* an unstable position. And that instability or unsureness is a gift. So let's not be too quick to make people stable, to make them concrete, concretized.

An appropriate amount of instability is the ground for new growth. In oscillating between horizontality and verticality, between increased connection and decreased connection, I express myself by impressing myself on the world, and I allow the world to impress upon me as it expresses itself. And in that process of to and fro, of out to the world and back from the world, I am born and formed.

The horizontality of animals permits them only one role. The human phenomenon of verticality allows for the formation of many roles. The ability to create and maintain roles enlarges our range of expression. It's our capacity for assuming specific roles in specific situations that safeguards our freedom. Being upright generates a surplus of energy, which we either bind rigidly in the form of contractions and stereotypes for alleviating anxiety or which we use in the manufacture of a role designed to bring us appropriate contact and pleasure at this time. If we go the route of contact and pleasure, we funnel and channel our energy into an expressive role until that role is no longer useful. The amount of free energy available to us correlates with the diversity of our roles.

When our role becomes fixed or stereotyped, it works against us. It's then that it becomes a defense system that maintains ritualized and compulsive boundaries. All of us create boundaries in order to survive. But when we find these boundaries no longer necessary, we dismantle them. Oftentimes we need others to help us do this. Asking for help doesn't mean that we are sick. Nobody has ever convinced me that life is sick.

If we experience how we reach out to the larger

world and come back to our bodily world, if we experience how we reach out to others and return to ourselves, if we perceive how our hungers are aroused and how we satisfy them, if we become aware of which roles are active when, we will learn our bodily rhythms, enhance our self-regulation. We will begin to participate in making the unconscious conscious, in transforming perceptions into actions, in making the unknown known and the unexpressed expressed. We won't be perfect, but we'll be more loving of ourselves and our life. We will incarnate ourselves, manifest ourselves as bodies in our world.

Afterword

One finds in this book what has happened to Stanley Keleman as a man: not a technique, not a therapeutic model, but the search for a way of standing in America and history. The nature of that search depends not only on Stanley's nature and the nature of the age, but also upon the tradition behind it, and so it makes sense to point out what that tradition is: the thrust of thought which begins with Freud and emerges fully in Reich before passing through Lowen's bio-energetics and into Stanely's work. Despite changes in emphasis and harmonies there is always a particular slant to that tradition, a basic tone: an insistent restoration of animal being, the localization within the self of a living universe.

Reich is the key. His work is the forcing of Freudian thought into the body. Something solitary and grand in it survives the debatable theories of his later years and the grandiose cosmologies. Even his most excessive statements are imaginative hunches which reveal, though mistaken, where to look for the truth.

Freud began it all, restoring sex to the center, reviewing our inner and social lives, renewing and revealing the animal past. Reich moved a step forward, tracing out the implications of Freudian thought, locating and localizing libido, *finding it*, moving the center down from the head into the body, making the richness of animal being the measure of health. Freud bent willingly to the "reality principle" and the need for intelligent repression. But Reich stubbornly held against them a vision of genital being. He demanded the absolute transformation of society to receive intact the animal energies of men and women.

Lowen, Reich's pupil and one of Stanley's teachers, took still another step. Or perhaps he took two: one step forward and one to the side. He modulated Reich's absolutism to a more restrained approach to "pleasure." Common sense returned. The principles of reality and adjustment reasserted themselves. Lowen accepted the tension between involuntary animal needs and half-voluntary social bonds. There is a pragmatic reasonableness to it all, a necessary reaction to Reich's driven excess. Once more the therapeutic vision is directed to the daily lives of men and women and the details of existence. But that necessary correction also involves a reduction in size and scope. What is put aside for a time is the incomplete but cosmic vision driving both Freud and Reich, the prophetic hope of recreating entirely the way we see and move through the world.

That is the vision renewed in Stanley's work. But it is given a new direction. There is an attempt to understand the reality principle in a new way. "Reality" ceases to be a given, as it is with Freud, Reich, and Lowen. It is understood as *an underlying and continuous process: a biological and evolutionary event occurring perpetually within and around us.* It is a tenuous and changing totality: not only the remissions and taboos of culture, but also the evolving *nature* of men and women, a cellular process occurring at the center of each person and cell. Where Freud and Reich restored the body's past by revealing how it is held in the mind and flesh, another direction is now returned to it: the future. What is added is the dimension of time and the process of becoming. Both Freud and Reich were after "hidden" realities; for Freud it was the repressed parts of consciousness, for Reich, the body's abandoned energies. But Stanley's work is meant to be a way of *creating* a reality or, rather, of releasing in the body the energies needed to create a reality. We are no longer seen as the passive recipients of reality or of the past. We are, instead, bridges. We carry the future in our tissues and genes, and we create it in our lives.

Seen in this way, tension and dis-ease are not accepted (as in Freud) as necessary evils, nor rejected (as in Reich) as the tragic cost of an "emotional plague." They are perceived instead as recurring states of evolutionary change or as responses to social conditions. Reality is understood as a field extending both outward and inward in space and time. Our condition is not the result of some broken "relation" to reality; it *is* reality, a condition of growth through which we move. It is both scary and exhausting, but there is nothing to escape. That is simply how nature, culture, and consciousness work: in a series of unpredictable folds, jumps, correspondences, distances, illusions, echoes and parentheses all of it part of process, all of it "reality."

All this, I take it, is the thrust at the moment of Stanley's thought. The characterological work softens, returns from idealism to the body, but at the same time the concept of "body" is extended to include the moral, social and imaginative realms: the person. One escapes the tyranny of the therapeutic by moving beyond the ideas of health and cure. Therapy melts into philosophy and an implicit morality, but that, after all, is where it began and where it naturally seems to go. The physical techniques are only part of a larger vision of what it means to move through the world knowingly, lovingly and as a vessel for energy and force: a force in the world.

Stanley studied with Graf Durckheim in Germany and in the school of Medhard Boss in Switzerland. Durckheim worked with Kohler and Wertheim, and studied Zen for twelve years in Japan. Boss combined Freud and Heidegger in his work, mixing psychoanalysis with existential metaphysics. These are the obvious philosophic elements in Stanley's work, and other elements feed into it, and what emerges from it all is novel and yet in some way also older-fashioned: a grafting of original thought and avant-garde analysis to a European tradition of privacy, modesty and responsibility. There are strains in it of deep conservatism and patriarchal mysticism, an earthy but highly rationalized cultural style—a clear-cut moral philosophy held against the thin enthusiasms of the human potential movement. In its celebration of private life, its uneasiness with transcendence, its sense of flesh reality and physical being and personal choice, his work is similar in its modern way to an eccentric kind of Hassidism: a reverence for life centered in and flowing from the body's grace.

I remember watching Stanley work with a middle-aged priest. The man was working upright at a bed's edge, straining to release the energy and rage held in his upper body. He was pounding on the bed, his fists drawn together as if holding an imaginary ax, stretching upward on the balls of his feet, pulling his body back and up, then bringing his weight forward and down and pounding on the bed. It didn't work. There was no fluidity to the motion, no grace, no strength. The downstrokes were artificial and forced. Only when his weight was held up and back, body stretched away from the ground, did the priest seem real. At that moment—shoulders pulled back, arms held over his head and immobile, face frozen into a grimace—he was fixed in a powerful, anguished pose of crucifixion. But as he brought his body down again to pound the bed, the power vanished and there was only that feeble tapping at the bed's edge. Seeing that, Stanley had him hold his upright crucified position; had him breathe deeply again and again, had him feel the spasms beginning to run without control from his legs through his belly to chest and head and eyes and then back again, a tensed trembling, half defiance, half shame and fear. He held for a moment, for two, and then broke. He fell to his knees, head bent forward and touching the floor, sobbing, letting go, his whole body shaking.

His collapse was a kind of return: body to

ground, folded and humbled but also substanced, substantiated—charged and alive. I saw then what Lawrence was talking about in *The Man Who Died:* that crucifixion is the loss of contact and grounding, a lifting up and away, the self denied its ground of being and the earth, its relation to gravity and energy. Doubled over, the priest was once again in touch, pressing one hand to the ground and the other into his own belly: embryonic, enfolded and infolding. Later he said that it was the first time in months he had cried or prayed; that he had been awed by a sense of humility in the presence of enveloping power—the feeling he had first felt years ago when called.

The sense of returning is a renewal of the body's habitation: *a redemption.* It is the heart of any decent healing. It is not unconnected to liberation, but it is deeper, sweeter, and closer to the bone of change. If liberation is breaking free, redemption is a coming home: a sense of location, of ease and belonging, of potency. It is not an escape or release, but a descent into the body, an entrance into the sweet swift currents Blake called "the river of life." In that, Stanley's work reminds me in some ways of that of the Hassids, who wanted always to "reveal God in this low undermost world, in man, that in him there be no limb and no movement in which God's strength might not be hidden, and none with which he could not accomplish unification." *Accomplish* unification. That is it exactly. Unification is neither an "event" nor a utopian condition waiting to be entered. It is a task: something we succeed or fail in doing with every gesture, word and thought, depending solely on the nature of the act, our underlying passion and receptivity.

I can also remember watching Stanley work with a woman, forty-five, red-faced, something in her of the top-sergeant: a harsh and raspy voice, an unconvincingly cheerful and aggressive manner. She had worked with Stanley before, and there was a camaraderie between them as she worked on the bed to get at, to get at—what? To get at the lost power and sweetness of the body, to set flowing again the life now only in the mind and lost to the body. The reasons for that loss are multifold, and they do not really matter here; what matters is what happened then: the sudden dissolution of what a therapist calls "blocks," the tentative nibbling tremors in the body, the belly and buttocks softening, the tremors beginning to take the body, and the ease of it, the gentle triumphant sexual waves, and Stanley, from his chair close by, murmuring "going home." What came from within the woman and into the room was a warm palpable light. One felt surrounded and filled by a honey-like sensuality. It was a movement of life itself, a filling of the flesh with life, the flesh *allowing* itself to fill, like a vessel.

Such moments are a source of vision, a taste of the natural condition of connected men and women. Whether a particular moment "lasts" or not is not the question. Nothing is lost, nothing like that. It is kept in the cells as a sense of what is possible, and it makes it possible for men and women to proceed. Stanley's work, in that light, is both more and less than a healing. It is a resignification, a restoration of mystery, a kind of awakening. There is an old tradition about the nature of paradise: one will taste its ecstacies no more and no less than one has been ecstatic in life—which is to say that the depth of the body's life is the direction of fate. Change, value, signification, renewal—all of these mean change in the body's field, a charging of the flesh: the reception in the body of the taste and pulsations of life.

In this sense, what Stanley does is a blowing on the sparks, a kindling. There is a tough pragmatic tenderness to it: the fierce gentleness of one who understands that beyond our fear and perplexity there is again fear and perplexity, but that we can also move from love to deeper love. Stanley understands that there is never any final "getting better." There is only a different way of being in the world, a steady deepening of reception the occasional and life-giving streaming of light in the bodies of men and women— their gestures and imaginings in the dimension of eternity brought back and down to their immediate lives, redeemed by them and redeeming them.

If we share any work as men and women it is just that: to make light of fear and deepen the day with the night's mysteries, to learn as best we can what we are and are not, what we can and cannot be. What we must reclaim together now is not the "future" itself but the thrust and depth of life in ourselves which steers and *becomes* the future. The future is never anything more than projection and hallucination. There is really *no* future. There is merely a tending, a current, a slant. The future is *us*, magnified and extended. Its graces and sweets are exactly—no more, no less—the graces and sweets we learn to find or create in ourselves.

Stanley's work is a part of that larger work, and that is its loveliness and significance.

Peter Marin

ABOUT THE AUTHOR

Published poet, painter, metal sculptor, author, group leader, therapist, Stanley Keleman is renowned for his powerful charisma and gentle humanity. Born in Brooklyn, New York, he studied with Karlfried von Durckheim at the Center for Religious Studies in Todtmoos, Germany. He was trained by Nina Bull, Director of Research for Motor Attitudes, Physicians' and Surgeons, Columbia University, New York and studied with Alexander Lowen, Institute of Bio-energetic Analysis, New York. He has been senior trainer at both the Bio-Energetic Institute and the Gestalt Institute of San Diego, California. He is a workshop leader for Esalen Institute in San Francisco, works in Berkeley, California, and conducts seminars and lectures all over the world.

The center for Energetic Studies, under the direction of Stanley Keleman, is concerned with the study of the life of the body. The Center's programs concentrate on the biodrama of our lives, with how the rhythms and cycles of feeling and need form our bodies and our lives.

The Center is located at 1645 Virginia Street, Berkeley, California 94703.